AMAZING

CARD TRICKS

AMAZING

CARD TRICKS

BARRON'S

CONTENTS

INTRODUCTION

You can purchase a pack of cards for the price of a cup of coffee. With these 52 simple items, magicians can perform thousands of unbelievable tricks. In fact, some magicians scorn more elaborate props, entertaining with nothing but a deck of cards.

★ The chances are that you have already experimented with the rather laborious 21 Card Trick, where a friend thinks of a card and you count out numerous cards into numerous piles, finally revealing the chosen card to the general indifference of everyone present. Boring! You will not find tricks like that in this book! Instead, you will learn how to make your card tricks EXCITING, ENTERTAINING and DYNAMIC.

★ You will need to come to grips with a few sleights (finger manipulations) but don't let that worry you. You can take it slowly, step by step. You will be taught a sleight and then shown a few tricks that you can do with it, allowing you to increase your skill and perform great magic as you go along. You will be doing great card tricks even after reading Chapter One – but please don't be tempted to skip chapters. Just curb your impatience and the whole world of exciting card magic will be opened up to you.

★ White gloves have been used in the photographs in this book just to make the steps clear to follow. You don't need to wear white gloves! If you do, the tricks will be MUCH harder to perform!

★ Why reveal trade secrets when it is well known that magicians survive by keeping their secrets? It is hoped that you will be inspired to follow in the footsteps of many self-taught magicians in the past. New blood is always needed to spice up the magical world. By reading this book you have made a commitment and shown an interest in magic.

★ You will learn to perform professional card tricks. It is great fun to fool people – not to make them look foolish, but to ENTERTAIN them by manipulating their sense of reality and suspending their disbelief. Welcome to the World of Wonderment!

THE LANGUAGE OF CARDS

All specialized subjects have their own vocabulary, and magic is no exception. A list of basic card magic terms used in this book follows, with an additional glossary of terms on page 126.

THE CARDS THEMSELVES

★ A **PACK** or **DECK** refers to the complete collection of 52 playing cards.

★ A **PACKET** describes a pile of cards that contains less than 52.

★ **CUTTING** a pack is the act of dividing the pack into two piles by lifting up a group of cards from the top of the pack and placing them to one side. You have now cut the pack into two packets.

★ **COMPLETING THE CUT** means to pick up what was the bottom packet and place it on top of the original top packet.

★ The **FACE** of a card refers to the side that distinguishes it from the other cards: 2♥, 9♦, 7♣. If a card or pack is **FACE UP**, it means that it has been turned so that you can see its face.

AFTERTHOUGHT

Cards with a linen finish are best to use. Cards described as plastic are too hard for easy manipulation and should be avoided.

★ The **BACK** of a card refers to the overall pattern on the other side, often with a narrow border. Card magicians usually use a geometrical back design with a white border. Occasionally a trick will call for a card to be face up in a face-down deck. The white border on the cards ensures that its presence is not prematurely exposed.

★ **A FACE DOWN CARD** or **PACK,** therefore, refers to a card or pack that has its face hidden by being **BACK UP.**

AUTHOR'S NOTE

As with all magic books, this one is written from a right-handed point of view. If you are left-handed, I would still advise you to practice the tricks as described, rather than try to transpose all the instructions. A little ambidexterity will be an added bonus and give you extra flexibility!

A CARD SPREAD is the way that you offer the cards to a spectator for a selection to be made. The cards can be teased out between your hands, with your fingers extended beneath them to support the spread

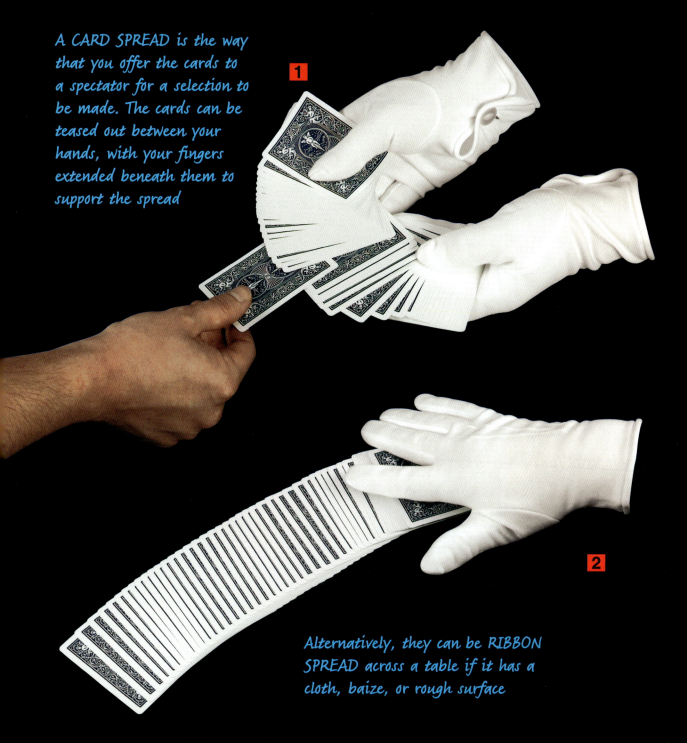

1

2

Alternatively, they can be RIBBON SPREAD across a table if it has a cloth, baize, or rough surface

LEARN TO SHUFFLE

Master these basic moves before moving on to the later sections of the book. Here, you'll learn to shuffle, and then to false shuffle so it looks just the same!

AFTERTHOUGHT

Work at perfecting your genuine shuffle so that when you cheat a little later it won't show!

1 OVERHAND SHUFFLE

★ Hold the pack in your left hand. Bring your right hand across and remove a packet of cards from the back section of the pack ("undercut"). Lift them up and over the front part of the pack. Pull a few cards off with your left thumb, and raise the right hand again. Repeat the same movements, dropping cards at the front and back of the pack, until the cards in your right hand have been exhausted and all the cards are now in your left hand. Repeat the sequence of movements above by undercutting again and shuffling off as before.

2 OVERHAND FALSE SHUFFLE

The overhand false shuffle is used to keep track of a chosen card or cards.

TO SHUFFLE, BUT STILL KEEP THE TOP CARDS IN PLACE

Put the four Aces on top.

★ Hold the pack in your left hand. Undercut the lower half with your right hand as before, and then pull off a single card from this lower half with your left thumb. At the same time slide it inward towards you so that it sticks out about half an inch over the edge of the pack. (This is called an "in-jog".) Then shuffle the remainder of the cards from your right hand in a slightly uneven way so that they cover the in-jogged card.

★ Your right hand now undercuts the deck again by pushing upward on the underside of the in-jogged card, grasping all the cards beneath it, and throwing them (still in one block) back on top. The four Aces are now back on top of the deck! With practice, the in-jog can be reduced to an eighth or sixteenth of an inch.

AFTERTHOUGHT

In magician's language you have just undercut the deck, in-jogged one card, shuffled off, undercut at the in-jog, and completed the cut.

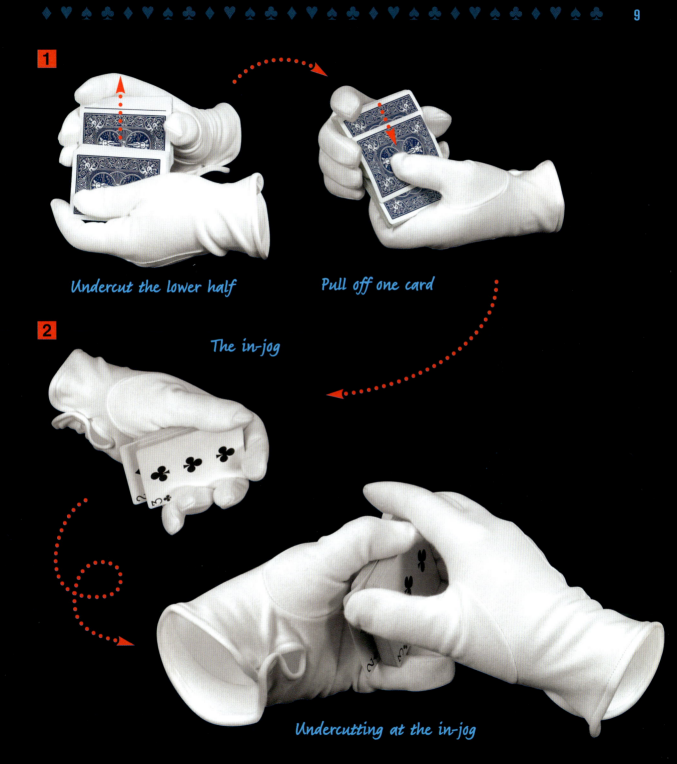

1

Undercut the lower half

Pull off one card

2

The in-jog

Undercutting at the in-jog

AFTERTHOUGHT

Spend a few moments each day practicing the routine below. You will soon be able to do it without thinking – almost without looking.

1 TO SHUFFLE THE TOP CARD TO THE BOTTOM

★ Hold the pack in your **RIGHT** hand. Pull off the top card only by dragging it down with your left thumb. Now shuffle off the rest of the pack on top of this card. The card that was originally on top is now on the bottom.

2 TO SHUFFLE THE BOTTOM CARD TO THE TOP

★ Hold the pack in your **LEFT** hand. Undercut the pack with your right hand as normal. Shuffle off the undercut cards onto the packet in your left hand. Hang on to the last card and deposit it on top as you complete the shuffle.

3 TO SHUFFLE, KEEPING THE BOTTOM CARD ON THE BOTTOM

★ Hold the pack in your left hand in the normal shuffling position but keep a strong grip on the face of the bottom card with your left fingertips. As your right hand undercuts the pack, the left fingers drag on the bottom card, keeping it behind. The original top half of the pack falls on top of it as the undercut cards are lifted and shuffled onto the left-hand cards in the normal way.

★ These simple variations on a seemingly ordinary shuffle will be the basis of many of the entertaining tricks you are about to learn. However, you must practice until you can control the cards smoothly and without labored concentration. It is not difficult. Remember that the shuffle must appear to be a perfectly normal one.

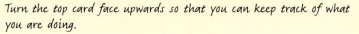

THE PRACTICE ROUTINE

Turn the top card face upwards so that you can keep track of what you are doing.

1. False shuffle the pack to bring the top card back to the top by undercutting, in-jogging one card, shuffling off, undercutting at the in-jog, and throwing the undercut packet on top. Your face-up card should now be back on top.

2. Shuffle the top card to the bottom and then back to the top again.

3. Shuffle the top card to the bottom. Shuffle again, keeping it on the bottom. Shuffle the bottom card to the top. Your face-up card should now be on top again!

After all your hard work it is time to reward you with your first trick …

1

Pull off the top card

2

Undercut the pack

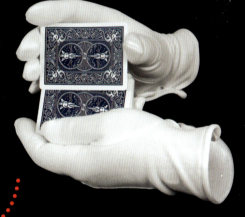

Drop last card on top

3

Holding back the bottom card

Now you're ready to practice your first trick ...

"X" MARKS THE SPOT

A spectator chooses a card and remembers it. He replaces it into the pack, which is then thoroughly shuffled. Somehow he manages to cut the pack to his own card!

WHAT YOU DO:

★ Spread the face-down pack between your hands and have a spectator remove any card that he wishes. Instruct him to look at it and, most importantly, remember the name of the card. Hold the pack in your left hand and undercut the pack with your right hand in the normal way.

★ Extend your left hand with the packet of cards face down and have the spectator replace his chosen card on top of this packet of cards.

★ Run one card from your right-hand packet on top of the chosen card and in-jog it! Shuffle off the rest of the cards, undercut at the in-jog, and throw the block on top. His chosen card will now be on top. Shuffle again, keeping his card on top, to accentuate the fact that the cards are being truly mixed up.

DID YOU KNOW?
Playing cards were invented by the Chinese, who also invented paper and money.

Place the pack face down on the table in front of the spectator.

★ Ask him to cut the pack in half. Then pick up the original bottom half and rest it across the top half as shown . Now you have to distract his attention!

"We have shuffled the pack and you have cut the cards. You could have cut the cards anywhere. Is that true?"

Grab his attention by looking him in the eyes. Now point to the cards …

"And we have marked the point where you cut the cards like this …"

He agrees that this is true.

"What was the name of the card that you chose?"

"The three of clubs."

★ Lift off the top packet and point to the top card of the lower packet .

★ Have him turn this card over. Amazing! Of course, the card that you referred to as the one he cut to is really the original top card of the pack, and not the one he cut to at all. By distracting him, he will forget the sequence of events.

AFTERTHOUGHT
This is a brilliant trick. Simplicity itself but none the worse for that. All good magic is 10% skill and 90% presentation.

1 The X cut

2

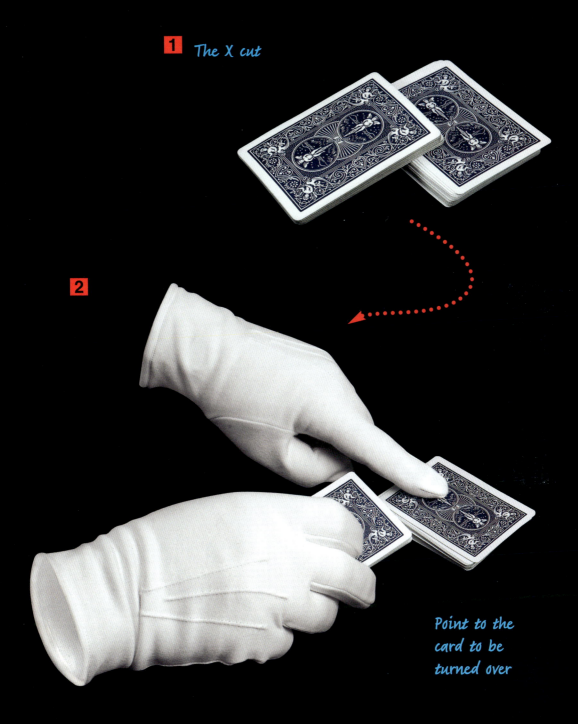

Point to the
card to be
turned over

MAY THE FORCE BE WITH YOU!

Many of the tricks in this book require you to "force" a card onto your spectator. By giving him "free choice" while actually placing your desired card in his chosen position, you can prepare some great illusions.

DID YOU KNOW?

The Chinese used playing cards purely as an instrument for telling fortunes.

THE CROSS-HAND FORCE

★ This is one of my favorite forces. The force card starts on top of the pack. We will assume that it is the 4♥. False shuffle the cards, then hold the pack in your left hand.

"I am going to do this trick without looking at the cards."

★ Put the pack of cards behind your back; as soon as they are out of sight, slide the card to be forced off the top of the pack with your **RIGHT** hand and slide it over the **BACK OF YOUR LEFT HAND**. Then cover the card with your right hand.

★ Turn around with your back towards the spectator and say,

"Please take the pack of cards. Give them a good shuffle and then place them back on my hand again."

★ When you get the cards back, turn around to face him again and slide the hidden card back on top of the deck. This only takes a second. Take care not to move your elbows more than is absolutely necessary or you will draw attention to the sleight.

"Did you really give them a good shuffle?"

"Yes."

★ Turn your back towards him again.

"Good! Take the card that you have shuffled to the top, look at it and remember it please."

★ He takes it and you have successfully forced the 4♥!

AFTERTHOUGHT

When you force the spectator to choose a specific card while appearing to give a free choice, you put yourself in a very powerful position!

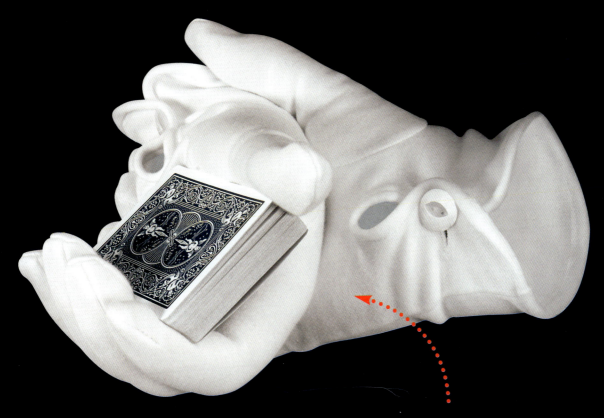

Your right hand covers the hidden card

THE GLIDE

The glide is another subtle sleight that enables us to show a card to the audience, deal it face down – and in the process, secretly change it for a completely different card!

PERFORMING THE GLIDE

★ Hold the pack up in front of you in your left hand . Your second, third, and fourth fingers are in direct contact with the face of the bottom card. You now apparently turn your hand over so that the pack is face downwards **2** and pull out the bottom card with your right finger and thumb, dealing it onto the table. In the action of turning your hand over, you simultaneously pull downward with your second, third, and fourth fingers and push forward slightly with your first finger and thumb **3**. By dragging the bottom card into this in-jogged position, your right thumb and first finger automatically come into contact with the second from the bottom card, and this card is then dealt onto the table as if it was the card just shown **4**.

DID YOU KNOW?
Originally, the face cards (or court cards, as they are sometimes known) were pictures of real kings, queens, and princes.

THE IMPORTANCE OF PRACTICE

The secret behind all good magic tricks is to practice, practice, practice!

1. There is no such thing as a bad trick – only a bad performance of a trick. Remember that constant practice and rehearsal will help you achieve perfection.

2. Don't forget, the method of achieving the illusion is usually just a small part of the whole picture – maybe only 10%. 90% of the success of any trick depends on your hard work, practice, and presentation.

3. You should never perform a trick in front of an audience before you are sure that you are really ready.

4. You must be so well-rehearsed that, if necessary, you could do the trick with your eyes closed! Only then will you be truly ready to perform it in public ... only then will your tricks cease to be mere tricks and instead become real, dynamic magic.

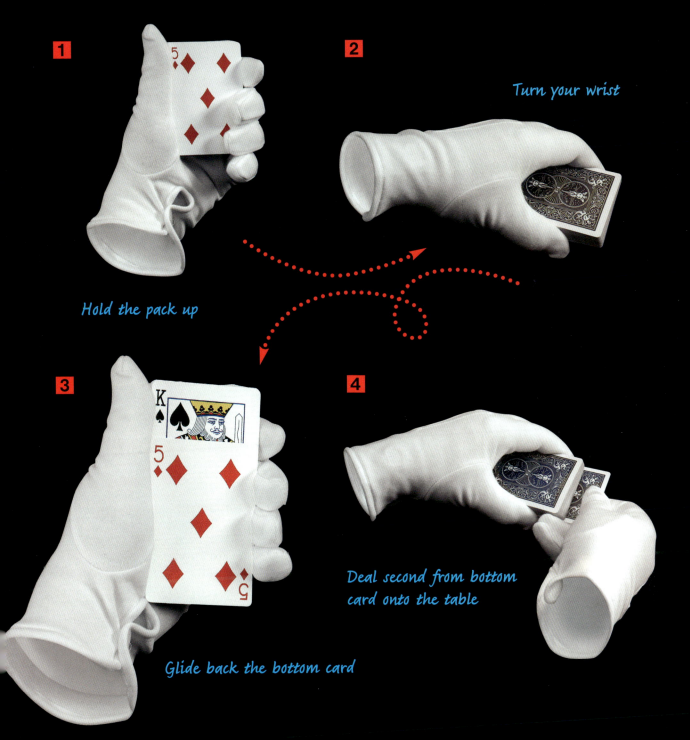

1 Hold the pack up

2 Turn your wrist

3 Glide back the bottom card

4 Deal second from bottom card onto the table

FLABBERGASTRATION!

There is no such word, but if there were, it would certainly describe this next dynamic trick! A spectator chooses a card. After apparently failing to find it, you produce a piece of paper from your shoe that has the name of the chosen card printed on it!

REQUIREMENTS

★ A pack of cards
★ A piece of paper bearing the following message:

> You are thinking of **THE QUEEN OF HEARTS** signed (your name here)

★ Fold the paper up and place it in your right shoe. Put the Q♥ on top of the pack and you are ready.

WHAT YOU DO:

★ Give the pack an overhand false shuffle retaining the Q♥ on top. Then perform the **CROSS-HAND FORCE (see page 14)**. We will call your assistant Clare. Throughout, remember to emphasize the fairness of it all – the fact that you cannot see the cards and that she has shuffled repeatedly, etc.

★ Ask her to remember her card before returning it to the deck and losing it therein by shuffling thoroughly. Turn around to face her while she shuffles. Now we intensify the deception.

"You shuffled the cards, Clare. You chose any one, returned it to the pack, and then thoroughly shuffled once again. Nobody knows where your card is, not even YOU. Is that true?"

★ She agrees. Take the pack back and look through the cards, apparently searching for her card. Remove any card that is **NOT** the Q♥ and without showing its face, place it **UNDER** your right shoe.

"Your card is now under my right foot! (Don't say "SHOE.") Please pick it up and tell me – yes or no – is that your card?"

★ She picks it up, turns it over and says … *"NO."*

"Oh, sorry! Let me have another try."

★ Sit down, take off your right shoe and have Clare remove the piece of paper and read out the message. Watch the flabbergastration on her face!

THE CHOSEN ONE

A chosen card is shuffled back into the pack. The magician has four attempts to find the card – failing miserably each time. The spectator is then asked to point to one of the four incorrect cards. When he turns it over it is shown to be the chosen card!

WHAT YOU DO

★ After the card has been chosen and remembered, overhand shuffle it to SECOND FROM THE BOTTOM.

"This is one of the most difficult tricks that I perform. Because it is so difficult, I will need four chances to find your card."

★ Spread the pack, with the faces towards yourself as if looking for the chosen card. It will, of course, be second from the bottom. From various parts of the pack openly transfer four cards to the bottom of the pack. The chosen card will now be sixth from the bottom.

★ Now hold the pack in the "glide" grip. Hold up the pack and show the bottom card.

"Is this your card?"

"No."

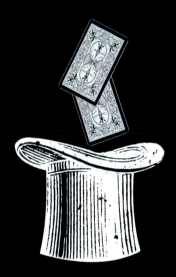

★ Turn the pack face downwards and pull out the bottom card that you have just shown. Deal it face downwards to your left.

★ With your hand still in the "glide" position, remove the new bottom card and place it on top of the pack without showing its face. Show the new bottom card.

"Is this your card?"

"No."

★ Turn the pack face down again and deal this card face downwards alongside the other card. Remove the new bottom card and place it on top without showing its face. Show the new bottom card.

"Is this your card?"

"No."

AFTERTHOUGHT

A magician is an actor playing the part of a magician. So ham it up! If you seem to believe the trick yourself, your audience will believe it, too.

★ Turn your hand over again and this time execute a glide – thus secretly dealing the spectator's chosen card, face downwards, onto the table next to the other two cards. Transfer the card that you just in-jogged from the bottom to the top of the pack – thus getting rid of the card that he has just seen!

★ Show the bottom card.

"This must be your card!"

"No, it isn't!"

Pretend to be perturbed.

"Oh, dear. Something seems to have gone wrong. We will have to change the trick slightly. Please point to one of the four cards."

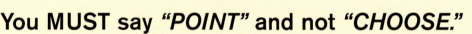

IMPORTANT

You MUST say *"POINT"* and not *"CHOOSE."*

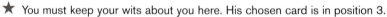

★ You must keep your wits about you here. His chosen card is in position 3.

★ Psychologically, he will point to this position 70% of the time! If he does, have him name his card and then turn it over himself. This will knock him out! What if he doesn't say "**3**"? What then? Don't panic! Here are your options:

1. If he points to card **1**, **2** or **4**, take that card away and have him rest a finger from each hand on the back of **TWO** of the remaining three cards. If he still hasn't touched the chosen card at position **3**, just take the two cards away. This leaves him with the chosen card. You have him turn it face up.

2. If one of his two fingers IS resting on the back of his chosen card, take away the card that he is not touching. Ask him to lift up one of his fingers. If he lifts his finger from the chosen card in position 3, take away the other card and discard it. Have him turn the remaining card up after naming it.

3. If he lifts his finger from the other card, take it away, leaving him resting his finger on his chosen card. He turns it over after naming the card that he chose.

AFTERTHOUGHT

If you keep your head, you can't lose here. Magicians call this forcing technique "Equivoke." Just remember to say "point" and not "choose."

DIG DEEP

A card is chosen and remembered, shuffled back into the pack and the pack is put into the spectator's pocket. He then calls out any number under 20. You reach into his pocket the chosen number of times, removing a card each time. The final card that you remove is the chosen card.

WHAT YOU DO

★ Spread the cards for a selection to be made. Emphasize that the spectator should remember his card. When he returns it to the pack, you control the card to the top of the deck in the course of your overhand shuffle.

"This is one of the hardest tricks that I ever perform because I am about to find your chosen card using only my sensitive fingertips. I would now like you to empty the breast pocket of your jacket (or shirt) and place the pack of cards in it."

★ Watch carefully as he does this so that you know which way he puts the pack in (that is, faces out or backs out).

"You now have the pack in your pocket. I want you to call out any number under twenty."

"Twelve."

"Okay. I will remove twelve cards from your pocket and the twelfth one will be the card that you chose!"

★ Begin to remove cards from his pocket, taking them from the **BOTTOM** of the pack. Remove the twelfth card from the **TOP** – this will be his chosen card. Hold it up, with the back towards the spectator and ask him to name his card. Slowly and dramatically turn the card around to show that your "sensitive fingertips" have successfully found his card!

♥ ♠ AFTERTHOUGHT

You do not need to know what the card is, only where it is! This simple trick has a dramatic effect because the cards seem to be out of your control.

♣ ♦

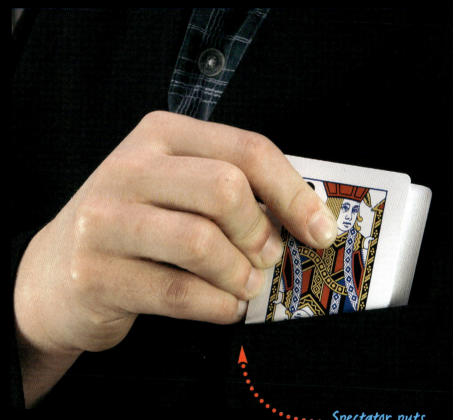

*Spectator puts
the cards into his
breast pocket*

THE LAZY MAGICIAN

The spectator cuts the pack into four piles. To his utter amazement he finds that the top cards of the four piles are all ACES!

WHAT YOU DO

★ Start with the four Aces on top of the pack. Casually shuffle, keeping the four Aces on the top by in-jogging, shuffling off, undercutting at the in-jog and throwing on top. Do this in a very lazy manner, as if it is of no importance.

"I'm feeling very lazy right now, so I think YOU had better do this trick for me! Cut the pack into four fairly equal piles by dropping off one section at a time."

★ Demonstrate this – then let him do it. The four Aces will now be the first four cards on pile number four **5**.

"Pick up pile number one. Without looking at them, I want you to transfer three cards from the top of your pile to the bottom of your pile. Now deal a single card onto each of the other three piles."

★ Now have him return the pile to its original position and then pick up pile number two. Ask him to do the same with this pile. He then replaces his pile and repeats the procedure with the other two piles. The end result of all this activity is that, unknown to the spectator, he has dealt three cards on top of the four Aces, then shifted the three cards to the bottom and dealt an Ace onto each of the other three piles. Now you must build up the illusion…

"I'm sure that you will make a good magician. Do you know why?"

"No."

"You did all the shuffling and cutting of the cards yourself, didn't you? I didn't touch the cards – I left it all to you. That's true, isn't it?"

"Yes, that's true."

"Well, turn over the top card on each of the four piles …"

★ The **FOUR ACES** stare him in the face!

♥ ♠

AFTERTHOUGHT

Mastering and performing the overhand false shuffle once again transforms a simple mathematical trick into a magical gem.

♣ ♦

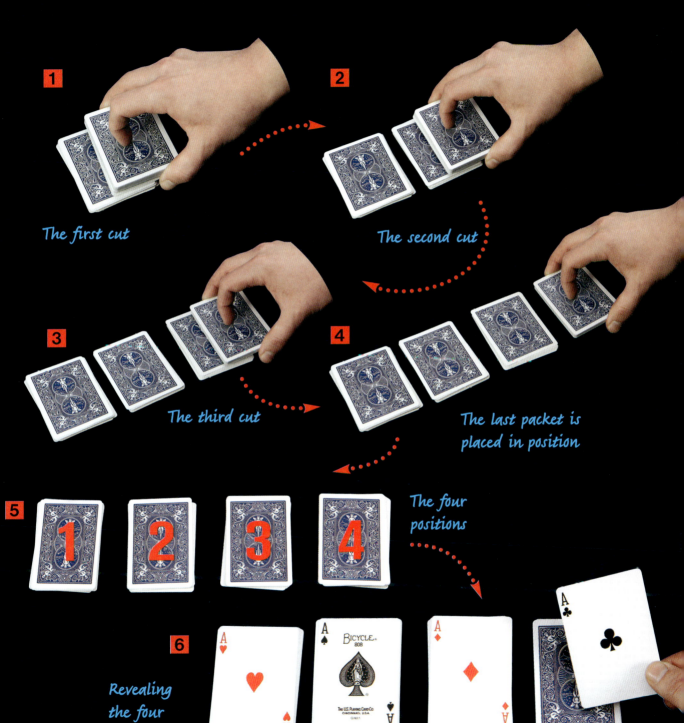

1 The first cut

2 The second cut

3 The third cut

4 The last packet is placed in position

5 The four positions

1 2 3 4

6 Revealing the four Aces!

WHATEVER YOU SAY!

A chosen card is shuffled back into the pack. The spectator is then asked to call out a number under 25. Say, for example, he says "Nine." His chosen card is found to be the ninth card in the pack!

WHAT YOU DO

★ Spread the cards and ask for one to be removed and remembered. Let's say it is the 9♦. False shuffle this chosen card to the top. False shuffle again, taking the chosen card to second from the bottom. **HOW**? Practice the moves as explained opposite.

★ Now hold the pack in the "glide" position. Casually show the bottom card, so that the spectator can see that it is not his card.

"You are not going to believe this but I want YOU to find your own card! Think carefully, and call out any number under 25. I don't want you to think that I am influencing you in any way. What number would you like?"

"Nine."

"Okay. Watch."

★ Turn your left hand so that the pack is face down. Reach underneath, pull out the bottom card and deal it **FACE UP** onto the table, counting,

"One."

★ Now glide back the next card and keep it in-jogged while you remove the next seven cards, one at a time, counting them as you deal them face up.

"Two, three, four, five, six, seven, eight …"

★ Now remove the card that you have been holding back and then deal it face down.

"Nine. What was the name of the card that you chose?"

"The nine of diamonds."

"Please turn over the ninth card …"

★ As promised, he has found his own card!

DID YOU KNOW?

Originally the suits of the playing cards were made up of flowers, wild men, birds, and deer, with an alternative fifth suit of lions and bears.

AFTERTHOUGHT

Your commentary is all important here. Allow your volunteer the chance to change his mind about his chosen number. It really doesn't matter to you!

Here's how. With the chosen card on top, hold the complete pack in your right hand. Place the pack into your left hand but don't let go of your right-hand grip. The left thumb rests on the chosen card, and the left fingers rest on the bottom card.

Drag the top and bottom cards into your left hand as you lift up all the other cards with your right hand. The chosen card falls on top of the bottom card.

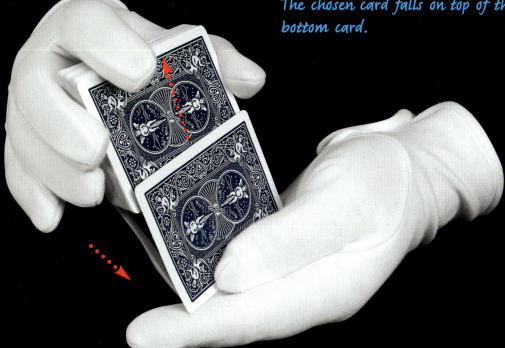

Now shuffle off the rest of the pack onto these two cards, leaving the chosen card second from bottom. Easy when you know how!

THE LIE DETECTOR

This is a brilliant trick and is completely self-working. The spectator's card is shuffled into the pack. The spectator is asked three simple questions, which he can answer truthfully or untruthfully. No matter how he answers, you manage to find his chosen card!

WHAT YOU DO

★ Have the spectator (let's call him **David**) choose a card. Have it returned to the pack and shuffle two cards on top of it – then a third card that you **IN-JOG**. Shuffle and undercut at the in-jog and throw on top in the normal way. The chosen card is now third from the top. **THIS IS IMPORTANT, BECAUSE IT IS THE KEY TO THE SUCCESS OF THE TRICK.**

DID YOU KNOW?

In addition to playing cards, the Chinese can take credit for the invention of dice and dominoes.

★ Give the cards a couple more false shuffles, then casually separate a packet of **NINE** cards from the top of the pack **1**.

The chosen card is still third from the top of this packet of nine cards. For the sake of explanation we will assume that he chose the 2♠.

"I'm going to ask you some simple questions, David. You may answer truthfully or you can lie through your teeth! Do you understand? You can lie all the time – some of the time – or not at all. The object is to make things as difficult for me as possible. Okay?"

★ He says that he understands.

"Now David, was your card an Ace, a two, a three, a four, a five, a six, a seven, an eight, a nine, a ten, a Jack, a Queen or a King? Remember, you do not have to tell me the truth!"

★ We will assume that he lies and says that he has chosen a Queen. Start spelling out the word "Queen" by dealing the cards one at a time onto the table in a pile – using one card for each letter of the word "Queen."

"Q-U-E-E-N." **2**

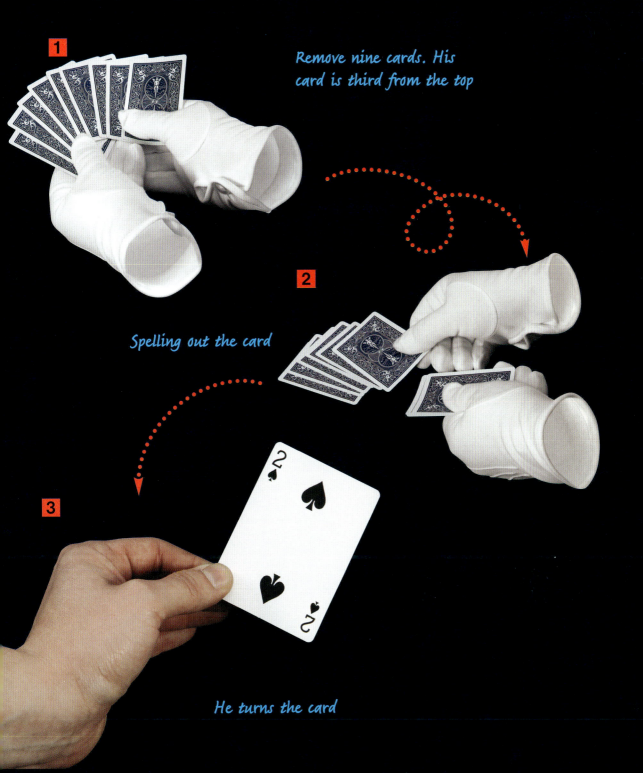

1

Remove nine cards. His card is third from the top

2

Spelling out the card

3

He turns the card

★ Stop after the fifth card (the "**N**") and throw the remaining four cards on top of the tabled pile. Pick up all nine cards again and spell out the word **"OF"** in the same way.

"O-F."

★ Drop the remaining seven cards on top. Pick up all nine cards again.

"What suit was your card, David? Hearts, Spades, Diamonds or Clubs? Remember that you can still lie if you want to – or maybe you think the truth might confuse me!"

★ David lies again and says, **"Hearts."**

★ You deal and spell…

"H-E-A-R-T-S."

DID YOU KNOW?

Americans began making their own cards around 1800. They invented the double-headed court card to avoid the nuisance of turning the cards the right way up.

★ Drop the last four cards on top. Pick them all up again.

"Now tell me – have you been telling me the truth or have you been lying? You still don't have to tell me the truth if you don't want to!"

★ He says that he has been lying. Spell out…

"L-Y-I-N-G."

★ The "**G**" card will be the actual one that he chose in the first place! Deal it face downwards onto David's outstretched palm.

"This time David, I want you to tell me the truth, the whole truth, and nothing but the truth – so help you God. What was the name of the card that you chose?"

He says **"The two of spades."**

"Turn over the card that you are holding!"

★ It will be **HIS** card – the two of spades! **3**

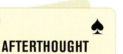

AFTERTHOUGHT

When you remove the nine cards, do it casually, without drawing attention to the number or appearing to count the cards.

HOW IT WORKS

★ The trick is infallible. The false shuffles enhance the trick and disguise the fact that it is based on a mathematical principle. Practice the trick by taking nine cards and turning the third one face upwards. Go through as many variations of the three questions as you wish and watch the progress of the face-up card. It always ends up as the last card, no matter what you do. A simple mathematical principle becomes an absolutely stunning card trick that will make your reputation!

THE PROFESSIONAL TOUCH

Well done! You've come a long way already, and have put in some hard work! Even this early in your magical education, you have mastered some exciting and dynamic card tricks. However, the joys and rewards of performing card tricks are only just beginning to open up to you!

In this section of the book you will learn:

★ How to make your card tricks look more attractive by peppering them with a host of flourishes, fans, spreads and catches. Magicians call this "the professional touch."

★ The killer technique of the DOUBLE-LIFT will be fully explored.

★ The beautifully subtle principle of the KEY CARD will be explained, together with its many uses.

★ You will learn how to secretly PALM A CARD out of the deck.

★ With these new sleights, plus the ones that you have learned in the previous section, you are now ready to tackle another NINE DYNAMIC TRICKS!

REMEMBER!

★ Bad performances are almost always due to lack of practice and rehearsal. Practice in front of a mirror so that you can see how a move looks from the spectators' point of view.

FLOURISHES

It has already been mentioned that 90% of any trick is presentation. To enhance the presentation and to create an aura of deftness, card magicians have invented numerous flourishes to add that little extra sparkle to the tricks. Just presenting a smooth riffle shuffle in the air alone can elicit remarks such as, "Wow! I wouldn't want to play cards with YOU!"

THE RIFFLE SHUFFLE IN THE AIR

★ This is not difficult, **BUT** it will require practice to perform smoothly. Hold the pack in your right hand with the thumb at the top end, your second, third, and fourth fingers supporting the bottom end, and your first finger bent so that its nail rests upon the back of the top card **1**.

★ Allow about half of the pack to fall forwards, springing off your thumb, so that the cards fall onto your outstretched left fingers **2**. The fleshy pads of your right fingers grip the cards and prevent them from falling on the floor!

AFTERTHOUGHT
The open display of elegant card handling can enhance your reputation and improve the presentation of your tricks.

DID YOU KNOW?
Americans made playing cards with rounded corners to avoid the wear and tear that square corners suffered from.

★ Put your left thumb on top of this packet and use the right fingertips to raise it into an upright position. Transfer your left thumb to the top edge **3**.

★ You should now be holding a packet in each hand, held in an identical manner and facing each other **4**.

★ Turn both packets face down and bring the "thumb end" edges together **5**.

★ Allow cards from both packets to drop off from your thumbs so that they interlace by about an inch as they fall **6**.

Once all the cards are interlaced, push all the cards together and square up the pack to complete the shuffle.

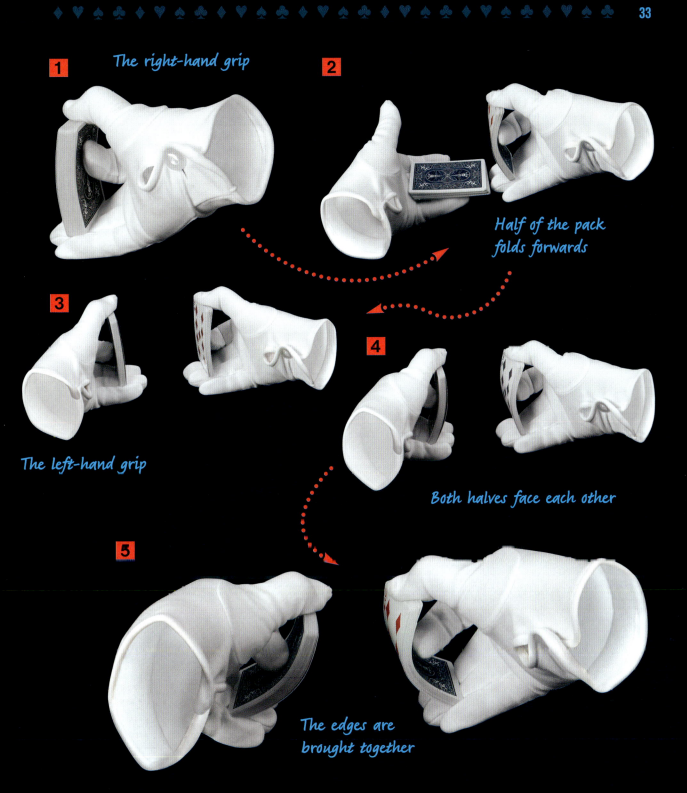

1 The right-hand grip

2 Half of the pack folds forwards

3 The left-hand grip

4 Both halves face each other

5 The edges are brought together

THE WATERFALL CASCADE

★ This is a very showy finish to the aerial riffle shuffle! When you reach stage of the aerial riffle shuffle, with all the cards interlaced, transfer both thumbs to the top card, at the position where it overlaps, and press down.

At the same time slide all your fingers beneath the cards, bending the outer edges downwards so that the fingertips touch below .

Now gradually ease the pressure on the outer edges of the cards, at the same time keeping up the pressure with your thumbs on top.

The cards will now fall separately from the bottom with a satisfying riffling sound and will cascade down, coming to rest on your outstretched fingers **8**.

DID YOU KNOW?

Before the advent of engraving, playing cards were painted by hand, making them too costly for all but kings and princes to afford.

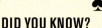

DID YOU KNOW?

The Joker was introduced about 1870 and used in the game Euchre as the highest card. Euchre was sometimes called Juker, which eventually evolved into Joker.

RIFFLE SHUFFLE CARD CONTROL

★ Most regular bridge and poker players use the riffle shuffle to thoroughly mix the cards, although they usually use the less spectacular version, with the cards remaining on the table throughout. It is not generally known that individual cards can still be "controlled" even when a riffle shuffle is used.

1. The top card (or cards) can be retained on the top simply by holding them back so that they fall from your **RIGHT** thumb after the final card has been released from your **LEFT** thumb.

2. The top card can be shuffled to **SECOND FROM THE TOP** by merely holding back the last card from the left packet and dropping it after the final card has been dropped from your right thumb.

3. The original bottom card can be retained on the bottom by letting it drop from your left thumb **FIRST** – before any other cards have been dropped from your right thumb.

4. You can ensure that the bottom card is placed **SECOND FROM THE BOTTOM** by letting a single card drop from your right thumb before you release the original bottom card from your left thumb!

Practice all these moves until they seem effortless.

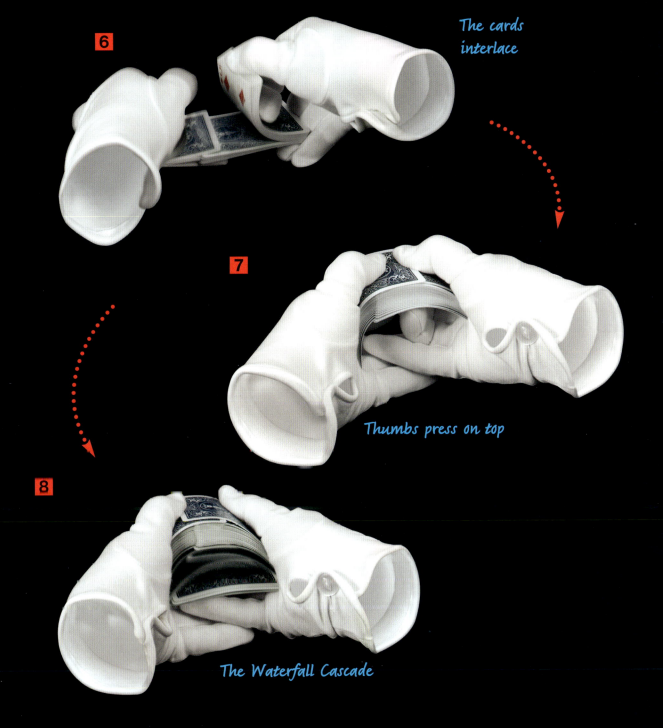

6

The cards
interlace

7

Thumbs press on top

8

The Waterfall Cascade

SPREADS AND TURNOVERS

You have already learned how to spread the cards evenly across the table for a selection to be made. The Spreads and Turnovers are very flashy variations that are guaranteed to grab the attention of your audience.

THE TABLE SPREAD AND TURNOVER

★ Ribbon spread the cards across the table, from left to right, as neatly and evenly as possible. The cards can be in a straight line or in a gentle curve **9**. Slip your index finger under the left-hand card and lever it up into an upright position. Continue to push to the right and the whole spread of cards will turn over like a domino rally. Put your index finger under the right-hand card, raise it to an upright position, then continue pushing to the left and the whole pack will turn face downwards again **10**.

THE FINGER SPREAD

★ In this variation, spread the cards, then raise the left-hand card to the upright position. Put your index finger on the "crest of the wave." Keeping a gentle pressure on this point, you can now "ride the wave" by moving your finger backwards and forwards **11**.

THE CARD APEX

★ Spread the cards from left to right. Raise the left-hand card to an upright position by slipping your index finger under the card. With your right hand, pick up the top card of the spread (the one on the extreme right) and use the long side of it to ride the wave in the same way you did with your index finger in the Finger Spread **12**.

A pretty touch is to stop halfway and lift off the card. With a little practice the pyramid will stay up. Replace the card in position and you can continue the spread and turnover.

♥ ♠

AFTERTHOUGHT

Always execute these flourishes on a tablecloth, since the cards need to grip the surface for the flourish to work well.

♣ ♦

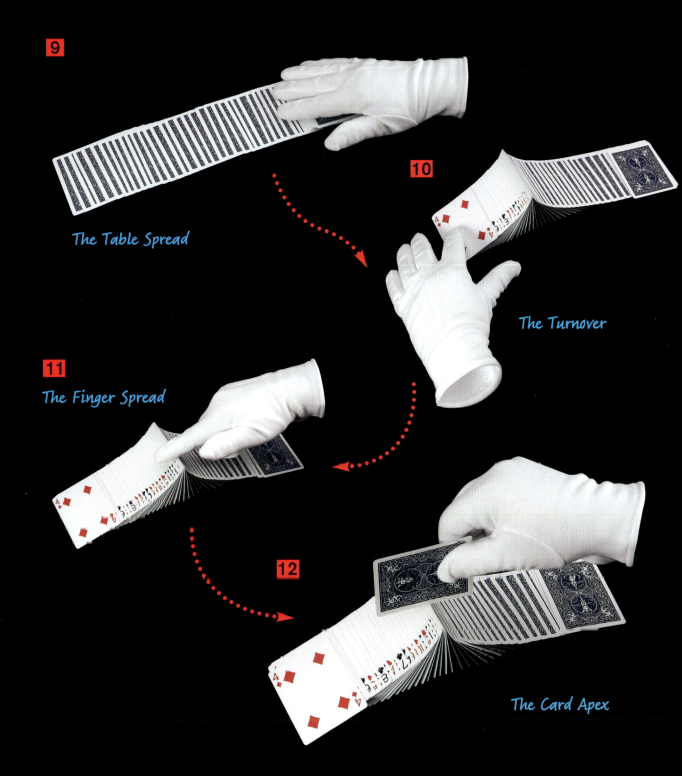

9

The Table Spread

10

The Turnover

11

The Finger Spread

12

The Card Apex

THE LENGTHWAYS SPREAD AND TURNOVER

★ This is executed in the same way. The spread, however, becomes longer and subsequently more impressive **13** **14** .

THE ARM SPREAD AND CATCH

★ Are you feeling brave? Having practiced the other spreads and turnovers, you might like to try this one. Try it with about half the pack until you get the hang of it. Hold your left arm out in front of you, palm upwards. Spread the cards evenly along your arm **15** , starting at the fingertips. Give your arm a quick upward jerk and the cards will jump into the air, still in a ribbon spread. Your right hand immediately thrusts forward to catch them **16** – like a crocodile snapping its jaws!

The Arm Spread

THE ARM SPREAD, TURNOVER, AND CATCH

★ You will drop a few cards on the floor before you get the hang of this, but please don't give up – your perseverance will be rewarded.

Ribbon spread the pack along your left arm, as before.

Now push the card nearest your fingertips upwards into a vertical position **17** . Continue to push and the whole spread will turn face upwards **18** . Now put your right thumb beneath and your right fingers above the card that is nearest your body. Thrust the right hand forward, along your left arm, and the cards will come to rest in an orderly pack in your right hand.

♥   ♠
AFTERTHOUGHT
Practice over a bed or a sofa so that you don't have so far to bend down to pick up the cards that you drop!

♣   ♦

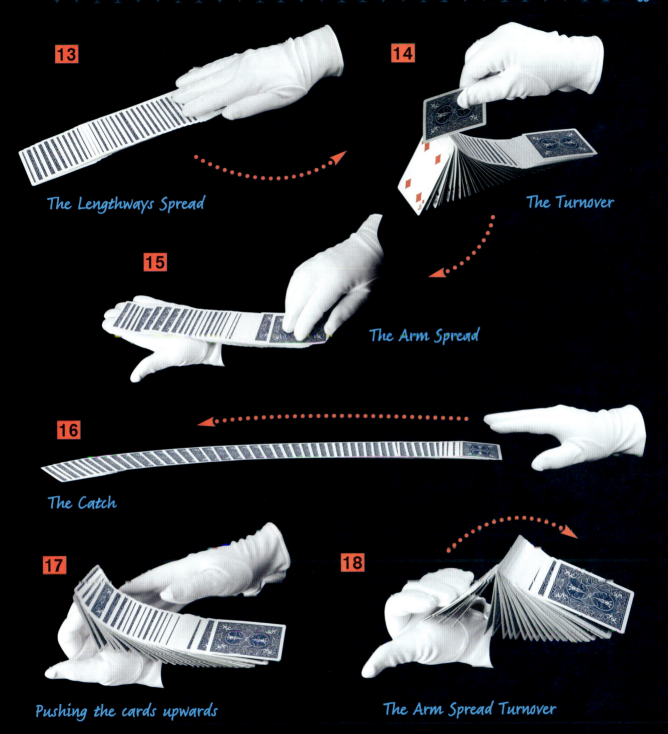

13 The Lengthways Spread

14 The Turnover

15 The Arm Spread

16 The Catch

17 Pushing the cards upwards

18 The Arm Spread Turnover

THE FAN

★ This is a very elegant way of presenting the pack for a card to be chosen. Hold the pack in your left hand as shown **19**.

Notice how the pack is nestled into the crotch of your thumb.

★ Your right thumb is placed on the edge of the pack **20** and, with a light pressure on all the cards, the thumb is brought around in a half circle to the right **21**.

Providing that you keep an even pressure, the cards will spread out in a pleasing fan, pivoting under your left thumb. The cards must be clean and not dog-eared!

AFTERTHOUGHT
Remember when you are practicing your tricks that new, non-plastic cards will always give you the best results.

FANNING POWDER

★ Some magicians polish their cards with a non-perfumed talcum powder (Zinc-Stearate). You can get this from a good pharmacy. The best way to apply the powder is as follows:

1. Distribute the playing cards loosely into a paper bag.

2. Sprinkle in two tablespoons full of powder.

3. Close the neck of the bag and then shake it for a minute or so to distribute the powder throughout the pack.

4. Take out the cards and polish off the surplus powder from both sides with a soft cloth. The cards will now spread and glide very evenly and smoothly, making all aspects of your card work more attractive.

★ **And now, it's trick time again!**

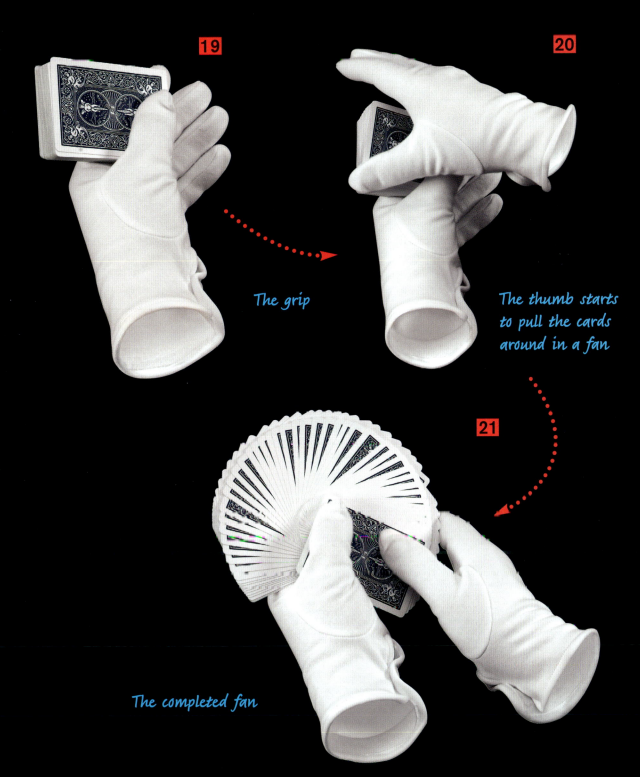

19

The grip

20

The thumb starts to pull the cards around in a fan

21

The completed fan

THAT'S IMPOSSIBLE!

A spectator removes and remembers a card, which is then returned to the deck. After a couple of riffle shuffles and numerous cuts, you name the card by apparently reading his mind!

WHAT YOU DO

★ Take the 13 cards of one suit and arrange them in order, Ace to King. Put pencil dots on the back of the Ace and King in the top left and bottom right corners. They should be faint – just strong enough for you to see them **1**.

★ Put the block of 13 cards in the center of the deck so that they run from approximately the 20th card downwards.

★ You are now ready. Spread the cards for a choice to be made, emphasizing the center section. Your dots will show you where the group is. It is vital that one of these 13 cards is chosen. Cut the pack at the point where the card was removed, to bring some of the sequence of your suit to the top, and the rest to the bottom. Have the spectator return his card to the pack. **THIS CAN BE ANYWHERE EXCEPT ON THE TOP OR BOTTOM!**

AFTERTHOUGHT

This great trick is only made possible because of the riffle shuffle (see page 32). It really does look impossible, especially when you ham it up!

★ Square up the cards, give the pack a riffle shuffle, then cut and complete the cut. Riffle shuffle again, then cut and complete the cut once more. These two riffle shuffles distribute the suit throughout the pack, **BUT** still in sequence.

Ribbon spread the pack face up so that every card shows. Look along the spread for the card in your suit that is out of sequence **2**.

Cover this action with a sweeping gesture with your hand as you say,

"You chose any card, returned it anywhere in the deck that you wished and the pack has been repeatedly shuffled and cut. I think you will agree with me that nobody could possibly know what card it is."

Sweep up all the cards and place the pack face down to one side.

"I'm not even going to touch the cards. Please think of your card. Don't say a word – and I will try to enter your mind and read your thoughts."

Ham it up, and then finally reveal the name of his card!

1

Here, you know that the chosen card is the 3 ♥ because it is the only ♥ out of sequence

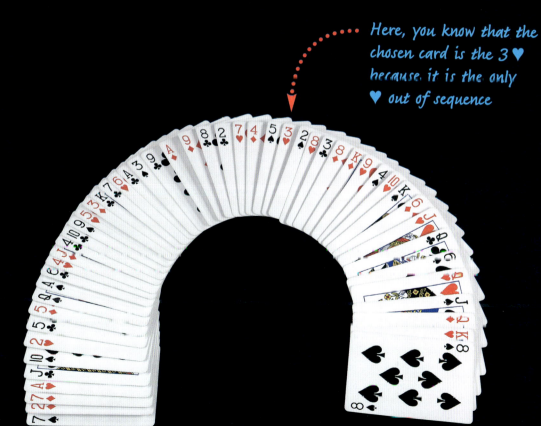

2

THE DOUBLE-LIFT

A double-lift is the art of lifting two cards from the top of the pack and displaying them as if they were only one. Magicians use double-lifts to achieve many fine illusions.

WHAT YOU DO

★ This sleight has two main uses. As the second card is shown to apparently be the top card, it can magically "change" into the actual top card by doing a **SINGLE LIFT** later on. The double-lift can also be used to show that a chosen card is not the top card – when, in fact, it is.

THE FIRST DOUBLE-LIFT

★ Separate the top two cards from the rest by slightly pulling them upwards with your right thumb **1**. Stick your left little finger in the gap **2**. This is called a **FINGER BREAK**. Reach over with your right hand with the thumb at the nearside edge and your second and third fingers at the outer edge. Your index finger presses lightly on the center of the top card.

Lift the two cards up as one and show the visible face to the audience. The cards are slightly curved **3**. Place the card(s) back on top of the deck and you have completed the double-lift.

THE SECOND DOUBLE-LIFT

★ Get a little finger break under the top two cards. Push both cards forward about $^3/_4$ of an inch with your right thumb **4**. Grasp the two cards at the protruding end.

★ Turn them both over as one **5**, and place them face up on top of the deck, making sure that they are still protruding slightly **6**. At this point you need to be very careful to ensure that the two cards remain aligned. Now you grasp the outside end again before turning the two cards face downwards and squaring them with the rest of the deck.

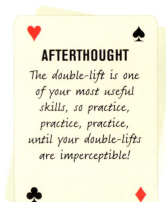

AFTERTHOUGHT

The double-lift is one of your most useful skills, so practice, practice, practice, until your double-lifts are imperceptible!

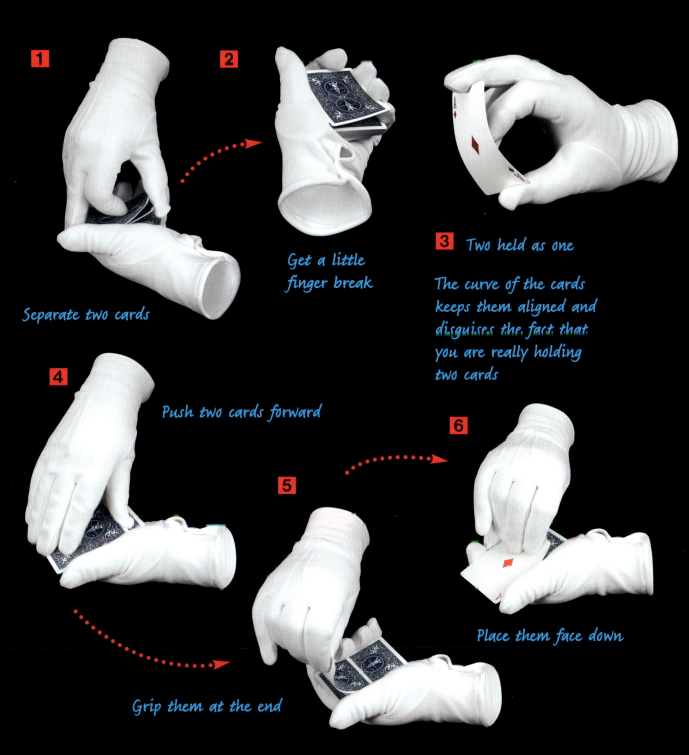

1 Separate two cards

2 Get a little finger break

3 Two held as one

The curve of the cards keeps them aligned and disguises the fact that you are really holding two cards

4 Push two cards forward

Grip them at the end

5

6 Place them face down

NOW YOU SEE IT,
NOW YOU DON'T

This is a great card trick, so please practice it to make sure you do it justice! It has a dynamic impact on the spectators and will be remembered long after more complex tricks have been forgotten!

WHAT YOU DO

★ A card is chosen and returned to the pack, which is thoroughly shuffled. Another card is shown and placed face downwards on the spectator's outstretched palm. The magician now taps three times on the back and three times on the face of the pack, stating that the spectator's card will now reverse itself in the middle of the pack. One face-down card is now seen to be in the center of the face-up pack. The spectator names the card that he chose. The reversed card is turned face up, but turns out to be not the chosen card, but the card that the spectator is supposed to be holding. He turns over the card that he has been holding all along and finds to his amazement that he is actually holding the card that he chose!

DID YOU KNOW?
The first engraved playing card was made by an engraver living in Basle, Switzerland, in 1445 AD.

AFTERTHOUGHT
A great trick is one that is easy to perform, is totally magical, and is mercifully short. This trick qualifies on all three counts!

★ Have a card selected by the spectator, returned to the pack, and then overhand shuffled to the top. Let's say that it was the 7♣. Explain that during the shuffle, the card that he chose may have come to the top. Execute a double-lift and place the card(s) face up on top of the pack with its right long edge projecting about three quarters of an inch **1**. At this point the cards are in your left hand. Let's say that the indifferent card showing is the 2♠. Ask the spectator,

"Is this your card – the two of spades?"
"No."

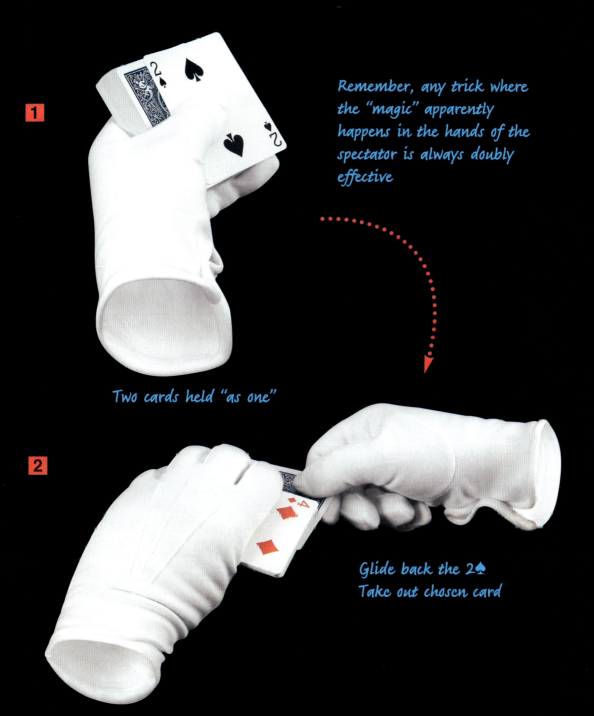

1

Two cards held "as one"

Remember, any trick where the "magic" apparently happens in the hands of the spectator is always doubly effective

2

Glide back the 2♠
Take out chosen card

★ Turn your left wrist so that the bulk of the pack is face up and the projecting card(s) face down at the bottom. Secretly **GLIDE** the bottom card back (2♠) so that it is flush with the pack and at the same time, push forward with your fingers on the visible card back (7♣) .

★ Take the card away with your right hand and lay it face downwards on the spectator's hand. Move his thumb to rest on the back of it. (Psychologically, this seems to prevent him exposing the face of the card prematurely and thus spoiling the climax.)

★ So – you have shown an indifferent card and, in the action of placing it face down on his palm, you have secretly exchanged it for the one that he chose!

★ Cut the pack while it is still face upwards, thus burying the card that he is supposed to be holding somewhere in the center of the pack.

The "dirty work" has been done. You only need to bring about the dynamic conclusion to the trick!

AFTERTHOUGHT

The double-lift, glide, and placing of the card onto his hand must be one smooth action. With practice, it becomes effective and deceptive.

★ After placing the card onto his palm you say,

"I will find the card that you chose like this. I will tap three times on the back (do so) *and three times on the front* (again do so) *and your card will turn itself over in the center of the pack."*

★ Start to spread the cards **FACE UP** between your hands to show the face down card in the center. (Alternatively, you could ribbon spread them across the table or, if you prefer, execute a neat fan.)

"Look! One card is now facing the wrong way in the pack!"

★ Take out the card and hold it in front of the spectator – back outwards.

"Now Sir, you are holding the 2♠, aren't you…what card did YOU choose?"

"The seven of clubs."

★ Show him the card that you are holding.

"Well I've got the card that you are supposed to be holding! What card have YOU got?"

HE TURNS OVER THE CARD THAT HE HAS BEEN HOLDING ALL ALONG AND FINDS TO HIS UTTER AMAZEMENT THAT HE IS HOLDING THE CARD HE CHOSE IN THE FIRST PLACE – THE 7♣!

THE KEY CARD

The principle of the key card is, unfortunately, well known to the public. As a magician, you should be prepared to take advantage of any situation – it is still possible to fool your audience with a principle they are aware of, if the circumstances are right.

WHAT YOU DO

★ The **KEY CARD** is the simplest way of locating a spectator's chosen card because no sleight of hand is needed. The idea is that you secretly place a card that is known to you next to the chosen card that is unknown to you. The pack can then be repeatedly cut. Complete cuts will not separate the two cards. You merely have to look through the cards and locate your key card. The one next to it will be the chosen card.

★ Here is an example of how to turn this to your advantage. Give the pack to a spectator and have him thoroughly shuffle the cards. Some people will accidentally flash the bottom card to you as they hand the pack back to you. This is a situation that you can exploit!

★ READ ON ...

AFTERTHOUGHT

With this, as with all tricks, beware of getting carried away with your knowledge. Remain calm and unflustered and keep your secrets secret!

I MUST BE CRAZY!

With this trick, we see once again how a false shuffle adds a clever touch, and helps to disguise the very simple key card principle. It's worth studying the commentary here, because it is deliberately misleading. Another trick of the trade!

WHAT YOU DO

★ We will assume that the bottom card (say the 2♥) has been accidentally shown to you as the spectator hands back the pack after shuffling it.

"You have thoroughly shuffled the pack, so I think that you will agree that no one – not even you – knows the order of any of the cards."

★ Spread the cards and have him take one and remember it. False shuffle the pack, keeping the key card (2♥) on the bottom. Cut off the top half of the pack and place it on the table. Have the spectator return his card on top of this half. Place the remaining packet on top and square up the pack. Cut and repeat the cut three or four times – emphasizing that his card is truly lost.

★ Place the pack face downwards on the table.

"I am not going to touch the cards – I just want you to think of your card. Concentrate really hard on it and I will try to pick up your thoughts!"

★ After some "concentration," pick up the cards and spread them in your hands. Look for your key card **1** and remove the card that lies **BENEATH** it. Let's say it is the 6♦. Place it face down in front of the spectator.

"You chose a card, shuffled the pack, and the cards have been repeatedly cut. Unless I can read your mind it would be impossible for me to know what your card was. Is that true?"

"Yes."

"What was the card that you thought of?"

"The six of diamonds."

"Please turn over that card." **2**

Watch his expression as he realizes that you have read his mind!

AFTERTHOUGHTS
If the spectator chooses the bottom card (2♥) to start with, you have a potential miracle on your hands! Go for the throat!

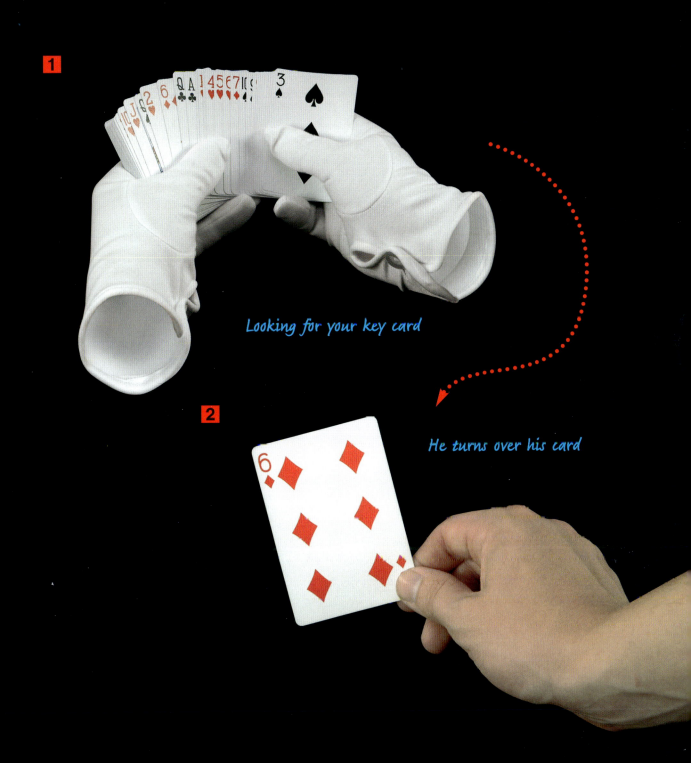

1

Looking for your key card

2

He turns over his card

REMOTE CONTROL

The title actually describes the method used to locate the chosen card in this beautiful trick. You find the card by "remote control" – a distant key card!

WHAT YOU DO

★ The spectator mixes the cards, chooses one, buries it in the pack, and repeatedly cuts the cards. The pack is spread face down on the table and you manage to pick out the correct card without even looking at their faces!

Take any card and put faint pencil dots in the white border on the back, in the top left and bottom right corners. Insert this marked card in the pack so that it is the 26th card from the top. Put the pack back in its case.

You are now ready to start. We will call the spectator Suzy.

★ Remove the pack from the case and place it face down on the table in front of Suzy (point **A**). Ask her to cut off about two thirds of the pack – **OVER HALF** – and place the cut cards to the right (point **B**). She must now cut the cards that she has placed at point B as nearly as possible in half and place the cut-off half at point **C**. Your marked key card will be somewhere near the center of the pile of cards at point B **1**.

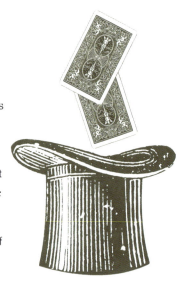

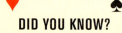

★ Point to pile **C**.

"Pick up this pile, Suzy, and shuffle the cards. When you are satisfied that they are mixed up, look at the card that you have shuffled to the top. Remember it and place it back on top again. Now put the whole bunch on top of this pile."

★ Point to pile **B**. Her chosen card will now be the top card of the combined **B/C** piles. Point to pile **A**.

"Now pick up this pile – give the cards a thorough shuffle – then place them on top of the other cards."

★ Point to the **B/C** pile.

★ When she has done that give the pack a complete cut and invite Suzy to do the same. Supervise this to ensure that they are complete cuts each time.

The pencil dots

The 3 position

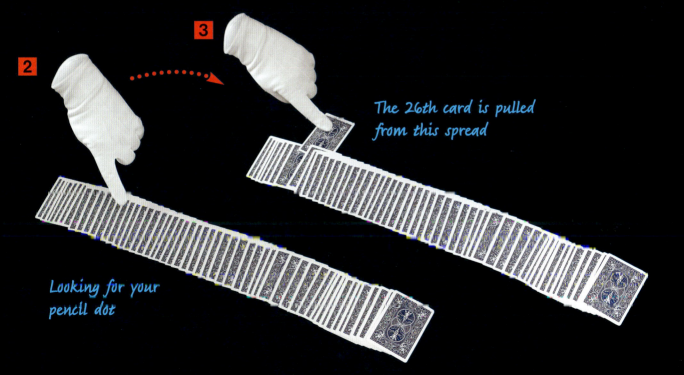

The 26th card is pulled
from this spread

Looking for your
pencil dot

"So far I haven't touched the cards. You shuffled, then cut the cards, chose one, buried it in the deck, and then shuffled and cut the cards again. It is impossible for me to know the name of your card."

★ Suzy agrees. It's true. You don't know what it is **but** you do know where it is!

★ Take the pack and ribbon spread it face down across the table from left to right. Make it as even as possible so that a part of every card shows.

"Hold my right wrist, Suzy. I am going to try to find the card that you chose by 'remote control' – a sort of psychic impulse!"

★ Extend your index finger and, starting from the left-hand side of the ribbon spread, slowly move your finger along the row **2**. Suzy still grips your wrist.

★ Look for your pencil dot and silently count it as number one. Keep counting to the right up to the 26th card. Go a few cards past it, then stop. Look puzzled, then retrace the path with your finger. Hover by the 26th card before dropping your finger upon it. Pull it clear of the spread but leave it face down **3**.

"What card did you choose, Suzy?"

★ She names her card. Let her turn over the face-down card herself!

AFTERTHOUGHT
If you reach the end of the spread before you reach the count of 26, just continue the count from the left-hand side.

AFTERTHOUGHTS
At first, palming will feel as if you are trying to hide a brick! Always palm when the spectator is distracted – either by their actions or yours!

PALMING

★ Simply stated, to palm a card is secretly to steal a card from the pack and conceal it in the palm of your hand. It is always done cunningly, with lots of built-in misdirection. Correct timing of the sleight is essential.

Hold the pack face down in your left hand. Casually out-jog the top card by pushing it slightly forward with your thumb **1**.

★ Bring your right hand over to the left and let your fingertips gently rest along the protruding edge **2**. In this position, the palm of your right hand completely covers the pack. Press down with your fingertips and the top card will pivot upwards into your palm. Arch your right hand slightly so that you can grip on the card, using only your palm and fingertips **3**.

★ Move your right hand to the right and grip the pack between your right thumb and fingers **4**.

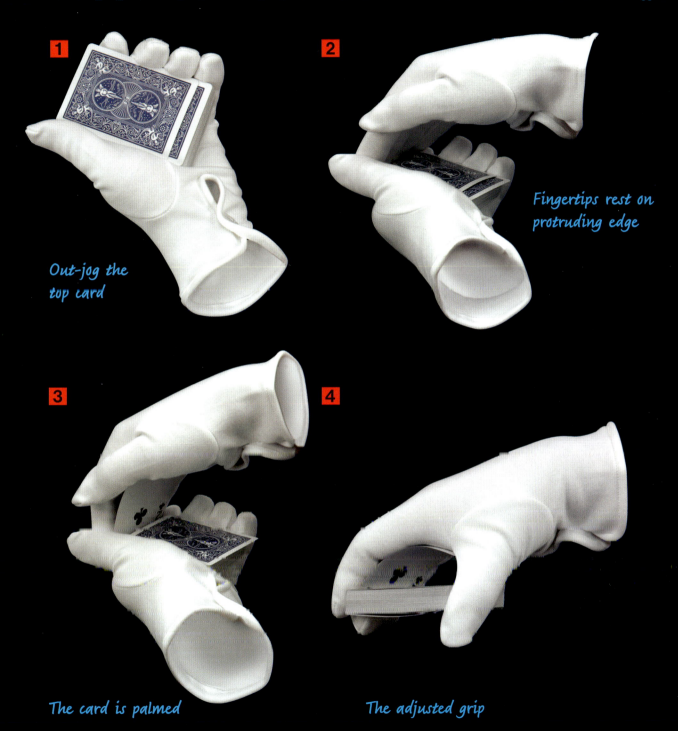

1 Out-jog the top card

2 Fingertips rest on protruding edge

3 The card is palmed

4 The adjusted grip

FORETHOUGHT

The key card principle comes into play again – only this time we use four of them! Four spectators think of different cards and you instantly find them by apparently reading their minds. You start with four "like" cards (let's say sevens) on top of the pack as key cards .

WHAT YOU DO

★ Sit four spectators in a row at your table. Give the pack a couple of false shuffles, keeping the sevens on top. Slip the top card to the bottom.

★ Deal the top four cards in a row from left to right, one in front of each spectator. Continue to deal cards on top of these first four cards.

"Would someone call out 'Stop' before I get to the end, please?"

★ You will have probably dealt five or six cards per pile before you hear "Stop" **2**.

"Look at the top card of your pile. Remember it and replace it, please."

★ The balance of the pack in your hand has a seven at the bottom. Drop them all on top of the left pile, placing a seven directly above the chosen card. Pick up all the cards in this position and drop them on top of the next pile.

AFTERTHOUGHT

If you can riffle shuffle, it is very easy to keep the three top cards and the bottom card in place. Just let the bottom card fall first and the top three fall last!

Pick up all the cards again and stack them on the third pile, and then again on the fourth pile. You now have a seven above each of the chosen cards.

★ Ask each person in turn to cut the pack. You complete the cuts for them.

"The pack was thoroughly shuffled and you each decided which cards you wanted. I'm now going to try to read your minds and see your cards! Please concentrate. Don't call out – just think of them."

★ Look through the cards with the faces towards you. When you spot each of the sevens remove the card that it faces **3**. Hold them up but don't show them just yet. Point to the first spectator.

"Sir, please name the card that you are thinking of."

★ He does. Remove the one that he has named from the four that you are holding and place it face up in front of him! Do the same with the other three spectators. They will all agree that it must be mind reading!

1

The four sevens on top

2

The four piles

3

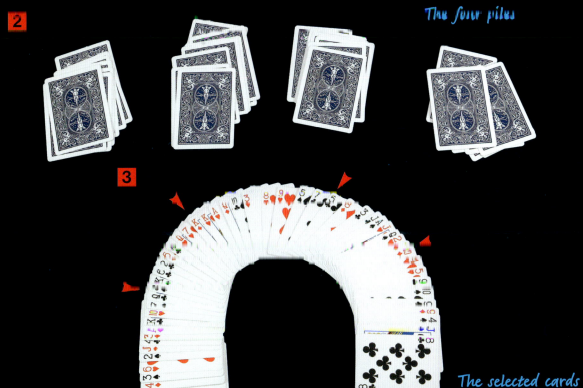

The selected cards

OUT OF POCKET

A card is chosen, returned to the pack and thoroughly shuffled. The spectator deals out ten cards, which are placed in your jacket pocket. You alternate removing cards, and the spectator takes out the last one. It proves to be his chosen card!

DID YOU KNOW?

A pack of cards is like an almanac:
52 cards = 52 weeks
4 suits = 4 seasons
12 face cards = 12 months

WHAT YOU DO

★ When the card has been chosen and remembered, you have it returned to the pack and control it to the top during an overhand shuffle. Hand the pack to the spectator and at the same time extend your left hand, palm upwards.

"Please deal ten cards onto my hand, face down, one at a time."

★ Count them out aloud as he does this. His chosen card will now be the bottom card of these ten. Put the packet of ten cards into your jacket pocket with the bottom (chosen) card facing and nearest to your body **1**.

"We'll reach into my pocket and remove single cards. You can choose any ones you like. Okay? I'll go first."

★ Reach into your pocket, remove the chosen card, and without showing its face, place it face down on your left palm.

"Now it's your turn. Take out any card – any card at all."

He does. You then take out another card and slide it underneath the one that you are already holding.

"Take out another one, please."

★ He does. Then you remove another one – sliding it underneath the other two that you hold. He takes out another one. You then take out a fourth card, sliding it beneath the other three. Now, get ready to palm the chosen card from the top of the packet of cards that you are holding.

"Please take out your fourth card."

★ Palm the card as soon as he starts to do this. He will be concentrating on the task at hand and the misdirection is perfect. He takes his fourth card and adds it to his pile.

1 *Put the cards into your pocket*

2 *Spectator removes the final card*

"I'm going to take another one…"

★ Stick your right hand into your jacket pocket, let go of the palmed card, and bring out the other two cards as if they were just one card. Place them on top of the cards in your left hand.

"Now sir, before you remove the final card, please tell us all – what was the name of the card that you chose?"

★ He names it.

"Take the last card out of my pocket and show it to everyone!"

★ He does – of course, it is the card that he chose! **2**

AFTERTHOUGHT

Ensure your audience cannot see the face of the chosen card as your volunteer counts them into your hand.

THE HOT CARD

You'll have a lot of fun with this one! You achieve the impossible, yet the method could not be simpler. The spectator freely chooses a card and returns it to the center of the pack. In an instant his chosen card becomes the only reversed card in the pack!

WHAT YOU DO

★ Ask your spectator to shuffle the pack. Take the cards back and spread them face down between your hands so that she can remove one.

"Please look at the card that you have chosen and remember it. In a moment I will ask you to put your card back in the pack, and then I will place the cards behind my back so that I can no longer see the cards."

★ While you are saying this, apparently by way of demonstration, you put the pack behind your back. While it is out of sight, turn the whole pack face up and then turn the first two cards face down . Bring the pack into view again, keeping the cards neatly squared up. What looks like a face-down pack is in fact a face-up pack with just two face-down cards on top of it.

"Push your card back into the pack – anywhere you wish."

★ She does as you ask. Hold the pack very firmly and keep the pack fairly low so that she doesn't see the bottom card. The illusion is perfect **2**.

"Because you have handled the card it should be slightly warmer than the rest. I will try to find your card with the aid of my very sensitive fingertips!"

★ Put the pack behind your back and turn the top two cards over again. Flip the whole pack over and bring it forward. Take your time over this – pretend that you are having a bit of difficulty at first. Ribbon spread the cards face up across the table, showing that there is a solitary card face down in the pack.

★ Push it slightly out of the spread.

"Wow! This card is too hot for me to handle! If I am right, this card will be the one that you chose. Would you please turn the card over?"

★ She turns over the one reversed card. **Voilá!**

AFTERTHOUGHT

This trick works best with cards that have a white border around the design on the back, because they make it easier to disguise the reversed card.

1 *This happens behind your back*

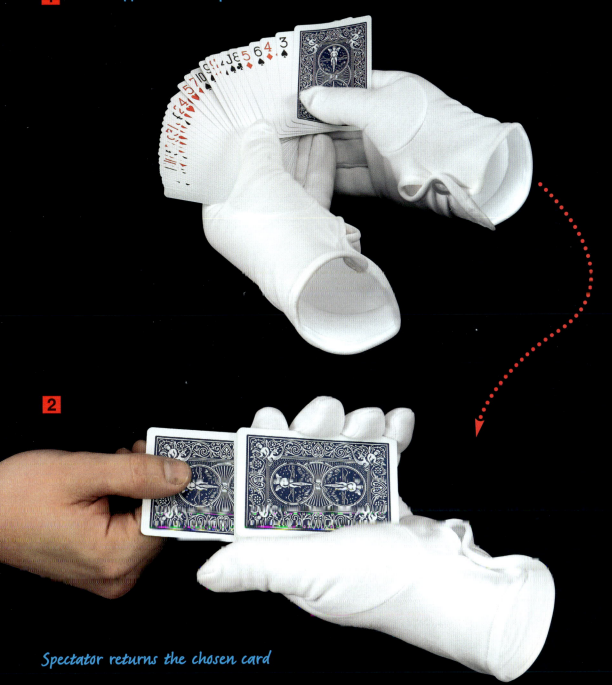

2

Spectator returns the chosen card

CARDS ACROSS

This is a classic of card magic. A simple palm, plus an abundance of audacity and a good presentation, make this delightful trick possible. Two spectators stand on their cards, but you make them travel through the air!

WHAT YOU DO

★ Get two helpers: we will call them Ann (on your left) and Tom (on your right). You stand behind a small, low stool holding the pack of cards. There is a table (or bar) behind you.

"Tom, I want you to deal ten cards onto the stool, one at a time, counting them out loud as you do so, like this: 1, 2, 3…"

★ You demonstrate and stop dealing after the third card – pick them up and put them back on top of the pack. Give the pack to Tom. He deals the ten cards. Pick them up and hold them in your left hand, leaving Tom still holding the rest of the pack. Start sliding the ten cards into your right hand as you count: *"Let me check these for you. 1, 2, 3…"*

★ Get a little finger break under the third card.

"…4, 5, 6, 7, 8, 9, 10. That's just right, Tom!"

★ Out-jog the top three cards and palm them in your right hand. At the same time gesture towards Ann with your left hand – which apparently holds Tom's ten cards – but in reality now only holds seven.

"Give the rest of the pack to Ann, please, Tom… (he does so) *…and then put your ten cards on the floor and stand on them. Now, Ann, I want you to do exactly the same. Ten cards please, out loud, onto the stool. Off you go."*

★ As soon as Ann has dealt the tenth card say,

"…and put the rest of the cards on the table behind you."

★ Gesture with your left hand to the table. As soon as Ann spins around to do this, you reach down with your right hand, secretly adding your three palmed cards to her pile, and in the same action pick them all up.

"Now, put your ten cards on the floor and stand on them too!"

★ Ann takes the 13 cards, thinking there are ten, and stands on them.

★ Now for the fun part!

"I need a long hair!"

★ Mime the action of removing a hair from the head of a nearby female. The more you "pull" the more seems to be left to pull out! When the invisible hair is apparently about eight feet long, reach to its root and snap it off. You must not touch the woman's hair – just mime the whole charade.

★ Press one end of the "hair" onto the top of Tom's head. Splay the hair out as you walk across to Ann. Press the other end of the hair onto the top of Ann's head. The tableau is now complete!

DID YOU KNOW?
In parts of India, card games are played with packs of circular cards with up to ten different suits.

"Tom – under your foot are ten cards; Ann – under your foot are ten cards; in between you is an invisible hair. This is what I'm going to do... Tom, I am going to make three of your cards invisible. They will crawl up your body and travel across the invisible hair until they arrive at your head, Ann. They will go down your back, down your leg until they arrive on the pile beneath your foot! They will travel one at a time and the first one will travel NOW!"

★ Pretend that you can actually see the cards traveling across the hair. Trace their course one by one. For the third card, make out that you are having difficulty with it. It could, for example, get stuck under Tom's arm. Have him lift his arm up to "release" it! From now on it is important that you do not touch the cards or go anywhere near them.

"Tom, if this trick has really worked you won't have ten cards under your foot any longer. You would only have seven. Pick them up from under your foot and count them, one at a time, out loud, onto the stool."

★ He finds that he only has seven cards!

"Ann you wouldn't have ten cards; you would have thirteen! Pick them up and count them out loud onto the stool!"

★ To really rub it in, you join in as she counts the cards – making sure you emphasize the extra three cards!

AFTERTHOUGHT
A simple palm of three cards creates a stunning trick. The misdirection for the palming of the cards is very strong, so make sure you get it right!

THE AMBITIOUS CARD TRICK

This is a bewildering sequence of acrobatics performed by the "Ambitious Card." The trick is unlike any other – it emphasizes the fact that sleight of hand is being used. You will get the credit for being a superb card handler – no one will play cards with you for money!

DID YOU KNOW?

In France, the King of Clubs represented the Pope and the Queen of Hearts, Joan of Arc. The King of Hearts represented the King of England.

WHAT YOU DO

★ Have a card chosen and remembered. Complete two overhand false shuffles, bringing the chosen card to the top. Ask the spectator to name his chosen card. Turn the top card over and show that it is his card.

★ Turn it face down again and do two more overhand false shuffles. Turn the top card over to show that his card has again returned to the top of the pack. Turn it face down again.

★ False shuffle it to second from top, by undercutting, running one card, in-jogging the next one, undercutting at the in-jog, and throwing the block of cards on top. Double-lift to show that his card has returned to the top again.

★ Turn the card(s) face down, take off the top card and push it into the center without showing it. Show that his card has returned to the top again! This time shuffle it to the bottom. Show the top card as if you have made a mistake – then casually turn the pack over to show the chosen card!

★ With the pack still face up, double-lift the chosen card and the one beneath it with your right hand. Turn the left over to bring the pack face down again. Lay the two cards (as one) face down on top of the deck. Take off the top card and, without showing its face, bury it somewhere in the center of the deck. Now show that it has returned to the top again!

★ Shuffle it to second from the bottom. Show the bottom card as if expecting it to be the chosen one. Turn the pack face down again and perform the glide – apparently dealing the bottom card that you have just shown onto the table.

★ Get the spectator to put his finger firmly on the back of it. Ask him to name his card again, and then turn over the card that he has his finger on!

AFTERTHOUGHT

As you gain more confidence, you can add more moves to this routine – although it is pretty good already.

SEVEN SIMPLY STUNNING TRICKS

With your newfound skills you are now going to amaze the public with seven of the best card tricks around – although you should probably perform no more than four or five at a time. Always leave your audience wanting more!

★ These tricks are a mixture of card subtleties and some magically enhanced gamblers' swindles. They really are simple, but they have been known to fool even an experienced magician!

★ Now that you're constantly working with your cards, let's have a look at these tools of the trade. Here are some words of advice:

★ Playing cards to a magician are like film to a photographer.

★ They are reasonably cheap and therefore expendable. There is nothing worse than performing a trick with dirty, dog-eared cards.

★ You must avoid becoming sentimentally attached to a particular pack.

★ Try to avoid handling your cards for more than half an hour at a time. With continued handling, your pack will get quite sticky and difficult to fan or spread. Open a fresh pack.

★ Professional magicians change their cards regularly and buy packs by the dozen!

★ Don't throw old cards away unless they are damaged. Keep them to make any "special" cards, or for duplicates that you may require for specific tricks.

SPELL IT OUT

Once again you demonstrate your card-handling skills to devastating effect! The pack is thoroughly shuffled and cut. You then proceed to spell out the names of all 13 different cards of a suit. Each one appears on call and in sequence as you name it!

WHAT YOU DO

★ Before you start, arrange the 13 cards of a suit in the following order:

3 – 8 – 7 – A – Q – 6 – 4 – 2 – J – K – 10 – 9 – 5.

★ Place them on top of the pack so that the 3 is the top card.

"Many people ask if I would be able to cheat at cards if I was playing for money. The answer is yes! But magicians are ethical people and only cheat when you know they are cheating! Let me give you a demonstration."

★ Overhand false shuffle the pack twice, keeping the block of 13 pre-arranged cards in place. (Just undercut about half of the pack, in-jog one card, shuffle off the rest, undercut at the in-jog, and throw the block of cards on top. It's just like controlling one card and just as easy.)

★ Give the pack a complete cut. Get the spectator to cut the pack.

★ Complete the cut. Your 13-card setup will still be intact in the pack. Spread the cards, faces towards you, so that the spectators cannot see them. Remove the 13-card setup and put the rest of the pack aside. Holding the packet of 13 cards face down in your left hand, transfer one card from the top to the bottom of the packet and start to spell: "**A**." Transfer the next card from the top to the bottom as you spell "**C**." Transfer the next card as you spell "**E**."

Turn the next card face up and place it on the table as you say "**ACE**."

IT IS AN ACE!

★ Do the same with the 2, transferring one card from top to bottom for each letter of the word. Deal the next card face up. It will be the 2!

Your pre-set order of 13 cards will enable you to spell out each of the cards from Ace to King and they will all appear on cue and in sequence!

AFTERTHOUGHT

This simple trick has been made into a very acceptable piece of entertainment by merely embellishing it with false shuffles and a couple of cuts.

1

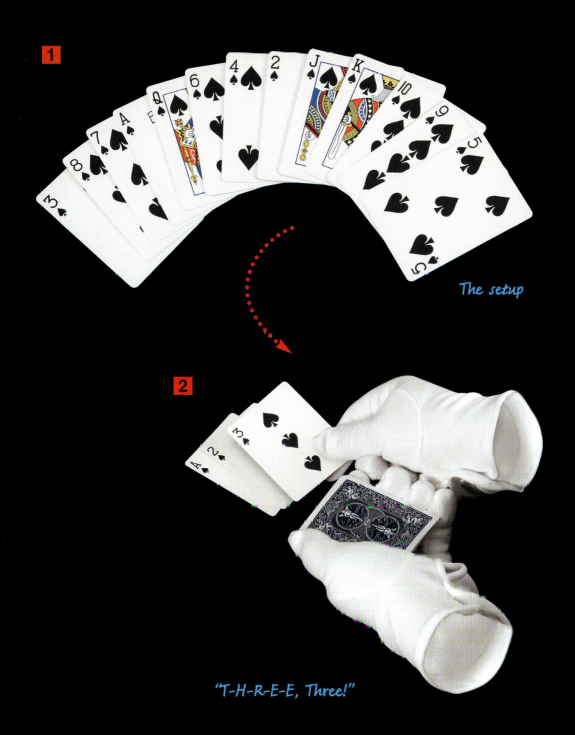

The setup

2

"T-H-R-E-E, Three!"

THE CIRCUS CARD TRICK

This little gem was used to swindle money from unsuspecting onlookers in years gone by. You claim that you can "read" the raised print on the cards with your fingertips. You are just about to make a costly mistake when you turn the tables in a very amusing way!

WHAT YOU DO

★ You use the bottom card as a key card (as in I Must be Crazy on page 50). Let's assume that your key card is the 6♥. It will now be directly above the chosen card. Study and practice the following commentary. You must deliver the lines accurately; otherwise the impact of the trick will be lost.

"I have found that, over the years, I have developed the most amazing ability to 'read' with my fingertips. I can feel the faces of playing cards and know what they are before I turn them over. Think of the card that you have just chosen and I will try to find it by using my sensitive fingertips!"

★ Start dealing from the face-down pack, turning each card face up as you place them in an uneven pile on the table. *"Feel"* the face of each one before you turn it over and lay it down.

★ As soon as you see your key card (6♥) you know that the next card will be the chosen one. "Feel" it just like the others, then place it face up on the pile. Let's say that it's the 10♦. Remember its name – but you must disregard it, and move on. Stop after you have "felt and dealt" four or five more cards unevenly on top of his card **1**. "Feel" the next one – pretend to concentrate – feel it again and then, with an air of confidence, say,

"Yes! I think I've got it! ("Feel" the card again). *I bet you $10 that the next card that I turn over will be yours – the one that you chose!"*

★ Having seen that his card has already been dealt, he will readily accept the bet, thinking that the next one you turn over will be the card in your hand! Put the card you have been *"feeling"* back with the cards that you are still holding, without turning it over, then reach down and turn over the 10♦! **2**

AFTERTHOUGHT

You should only use this trick for honest entertainment. Please don't take the money. You will give all magicians a bad name if you do!

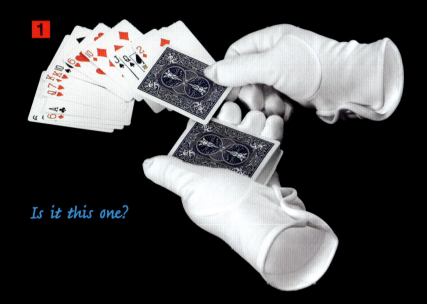

Is it this one?

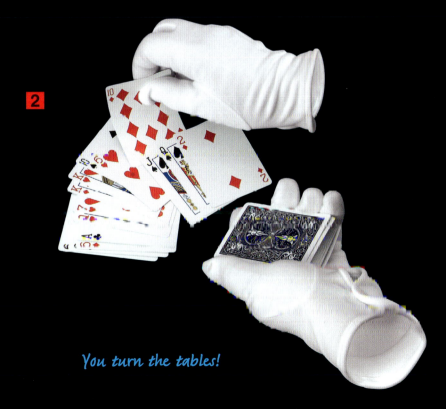

You turn the tables!

TELEPHONE TELEPATHY

A little bit of preparation is well worth your while here! Your spectator freely chooses a card, and phones your "mind-reading" friend to ask him which card he has just chosen. Your friend names the card correctly – every time!

WHAT YOU DO

★ You will need a telephone, a pencil, and paper. You will also need a friend who can be trusted to keep his mouth shut! If your friend is male, give him the list of male names. If your friend is female, give her the list of female names. Make a note of your friend's telephone number at the top of the list that you decide to use. Put the secret list in your wallet or purse and you are all set.

★ Your friend has been warned to expect a phone call. Let's assume that your accomplice is a man. Back to the performance…

"The fairest way I know of having a card chosen is to spread the cards out on the table and let you pull out any one that you want."

AFTERTHOUGHT

Prepare two of these lists, either by photocopying them or reproducing them on your computer.

★ Ribbon spread the cards face up across the table and have a spectator take one card. Obviously you see it. Let's assume that the chosen card was the 7♦.

"I don't know if you believe in 'mind reading' or not – but I have an amazing friend who loves attempting the impossible. I want you to phone him up!"

Give the spectator your mobile phone or, if you are at home, take him over to your telephone. Take out your wallet, open your secret list and say…

"Can you jot down this number…(your friend's number). Just ask for GEORGE. If he's there, explain to him what has happened and ask him if he can read your mind and tell you what card you are thinking of!"

★ Your friend picks up the phone and just says…*"Hello…"* The spectator explains the situation and will be absolutely astounded when "George," after "struggling" a little, tells him that he is thinking of the 7♦! All your accomplice has to do is look down his alphabetical list of names and find the name of the card that is next to the name that the spectator uses. "George" = 7♦!

YOUR FRIEND'S PHONE NUMBER

	♥			♠			♦			♣	
A	♥	Abdul	A	♠	Adrian	A	♦	Alan	A	♣	Amir
2	♥	Barry	2	♠	Ben	2	♦	Brian	2	♣	Bruce
3	♥	Carlo	3	♠	Christopher	3	♦	Clyde	3	♣	Cyril
4	♥	Daniel	4	♠	David	4	♦	Dennis	4	♣	Duncan
5	♥	Edward	5	♠	Ellis	5	♦	Ernest	5	♣	Evan
6	♥	Felix	6	♠	Floyd	6	♦	Frank	6	♣	Freddie
7	♥	Gareth	7	♠	Gavin	7	♦	George	7	♣	Giles
8	♥	Hamish	8	♠	Harry	8	♦	Henry	8	♣	Hugh
9	♥	Ian	9	♠	Ike	9	♦	Isaac	9	♣	Ivor
10	♥	Jack	10	♠	Jason	10	♦	John	10	♣	Justin
J	♥	Keith	J	♠	Kelly	J	♦	Kenneth	J	♣	Kevin
Q	♥	Larry	Q	♠	Lee	Q	♦	Leon	Q	♣	Lucas
K	♥	Malcolm	K	♠	Mark	K	♦	Matthew	K	♣	Maurice
JOKER:		Nicholas									

YOUR FRIEND'S PHONE NUMBER

	♥			♠			♦			♣	
A	♥	Abigail	A	♠	Alexandra	A	♦	Anna	A	♣	Arabella
2	♥	Beatrice	2	♠	Belinda	2	♦	Beth	2	♣	Briony
3	♥	Camilla	3	♠	Carol	3	♦	Cassandra	3	♣	Chloe
4	♥	Daisy	4	♠	Dawn	4	♦	Dilprit	4	♣	Donna
5	♥	Edwina	5	♠	Eleanor	5	♦	Elizabeth	5	♣	Emma
6	♥	Fay	6	♠	Felicity	6	♦	Fiona	6	♣	Francesca
7	♥	Gabrielle	7	♠	Georgina	7	♦	Glenda	7	♣	Grace
8	♥	Hannah	8	♠	Harriet	8	♦	Helen	8	♣	Hope
9	♥	Ilona	9	♠	Imogen	9	♦	Isabel	9	♣	Ivy
10	♥	Jackie	10	♠	Jane	10	♦	Jennifer	10	♣	Joanna
J	♥	Karen	J	♠	Kay	J	♦	Kirsty	J	♣	Kylie
Q	♥	Laura	Q	♠	Lena	Q	♦	Lily	Q	♣	Lisa
K	♥	Madeline	K	♠	Maggie	K	♦	Maria	K	♣	Michelle
JOKER:		Nancy									

SHERLOCK HOLMES

This subtle use of the Double-lift brings about an utterly perplexing trick. The Joker is taken from your outside breast pocket and inserted into the pack, directly next to your spectator's previously chosen card!

WHAT YOU DO

★ Start with the Joker as the second card from the top. Double lift to show the Joker to the spectator, then replace it (them) face down, on top of the pack.

"The Joker is the cleverest card in the pack. It can find anything!"

★ Take off the top card (the supposed Joker) and stick it in your pocket so that it sticks out a little . Give the pack a couple of false shuffles, keeping the Joker on top. Start dealing, face down, onto the table. The Joker is the bottom card of this pile.

"I would like you to call out 'Stop!' any time you wish."

★ He stops you after you have dealt a dozen or so cards. Ask him to look at the top card of the packet in your left hand, remember it, and then replace it. We will assume it was the 2♣. When he has done that, pick up the cards you dealt onto the table and drop them all onto the cards in your left hand.

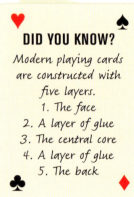

★ You have now secretly placed the Joker directly above the chosen card.

★ Give the pack several complete cuts and let the spectator cut, too. Square up the pack and place it on the table. Now take the supposed Joker from your pocket (being careful not to expose its face). With a great display of concentration, stick it into the pack. Give the pack another couple of cuts.

★ Make sure that the Joker is not the bottom card. If it is, cut again to bury it.

★ Hand the pack to the spectator.

"I won't touch the cards again. The Joker detective will now attempt to find your card. What was it?"

"It was the two of clubs."

"Okay. Look through the pack and find the 2♣ and the Joker."

★ He will be staggered to find the two cards side by side! **2**

AFTERTHOUGHT

For tricks that ask your spectator to cut the pack, always complete the cut for him, ensuring that the cyclical order of the cards is not disturbed.

1

The odd card goes into your pocket

2

The joker finds the chosen card!

ONE-WAY STREET

A spectator makes a random selection of a card. His card is returned to the pack, which is then genuinely shuffled. The performer could not possibly know the name of this card, and yet you find it instantly and infallibly.

WHAT YOU DO

★ The Ace, 3, 5, 6, 7 and 9 of hearts, spades, and clubs, plus the 7 of diamonds, all have a "one-way" face design. Take the 19 "one-way" cards from the pack and check that all of them have their tops oriented the same way. Place them on top of the pack, and give a couple of false shuffles, keeping the 19 cards in place on top of the pack.

"I've been practicing mind reading recently. I can't do it with the complete pack yet – I'm not that good! I will take about half of the pack…"

★ Take the 19 cards off the top and discard the rest. Fan the cards in your left hand and get the spectator to remove one. While he looks at it, close the fan from left to right. This action reverses the one-way design of the remaining 18 cards.

★ Fan the cards out again and have him replace his card anywhere he likes. Its one-way face design will now be the opposite way around to the rest. Square the cards up and give them a thorough genuine overhand shuffle.

★ Scan through the cards and look for the odd one out as you ask the spectator to concentrate on his card. Hold it up with its back towards the spectator. Have him name the card that he thought of. Slowly and dramatically turn around the card that you are holding!

AUTHOR'S NOTE

★ Although one-way BACK designs are not recommended for normal working, always look out for such a pack in your friends' homes. Rearrange them (when nobody is looking) so that all the one-way back designs face the same way. Ask to borrow a pack of cards. You can now perform "One-way Street" with a whole pack, using the back designs as your guide!

Turn any "one-way" card
through 180 degrees, and
you will see that the central
suit emblem is upside down

Closing the fan from left
to right reverses the one-
way face designs

BEAT THE DEALER

This delightful gambling demonstration will greatly enhance your reputation! The performer wins a poker hand and then lets the spectator win. He even lets the spectator choose the last hand, but whichever way the cards are dealt, the performer always wins!

WHAT YOU DO

★ You need three sets of three "like" cards plus one indifferent card. The odd card is on top followed by the other nine cards in any order. Let us suppose that you have chosen the setup shown here.

★ Our subtle secret is that whoever gets the odd card will lose! *"Most people say… 'I wouldn't want to play cards with you!' They are probably very wise. Let's play a couple of hands, anyway."*

★ Overhand false shuffle a couple of times, keeping the ten-card setup on top. Now deal out two poker hands of five cards each. The first card (K♣) goes to the spectator, the second to yourself – and so on until you each have five cards. The two hands are turned face up and you are seen to have the winning hand.

★ Pick up the cards, keeping the odd card on the bottom.

"This time I will let YOU win! Tell me when to stop shuffling."

★ Shuffle the ten cards repeatedly, keeping the K♣ on the bottom. Stop and deal out two poker hands again. Since the K♣ is the bottom card, you will end up dealing it to yourself as the last card. Turn the two hands face up – you lose!

"This time I'm going to win, but you can decide who has which card!"

Gather the hands up, making sure that the K♣ is the top card. False shuffle.

"Tell me when to stop shuffling."

★ Stop when asked, then deal the top card (K♣) in front of the spectator. Take the next card and ask the spectator whether he would like it or whether he would like you to have it. Continue in this way until he has chosen five cards for himself. The rest are yours. He loses whatever he does!

AFTERTHOUGHT

This trick is simple but effective. He will forget that you dealt the first card to him and that he only chose four of his five cards!

A FULL HOUSE (Any three of a kind plus any pair) beats
THREE OF A KIND plus an odd card and the K♣

Any THREE OF A KIND plus two odd cards beats TWO PAIRS plus the K♣

Any TWO PAIRS plus one odd card beats ONE PAIR
plus two odd cards and the K♣

ALIEN ABDUCTION

Very few card tricks have the impact on the spectators that this one has. The performer shines an "abduction ray" at his spectators, making their cards vanish, only to be found in the secure packet of cards that a fourth spectator has been guarding all along!

WHAT YOU DO

★ You need one and a half packs of cards, two rubber bands, and a small flashlight **1**. You must assemble a special pack of cards made up from two sets of 26 identical cards. In other words, the first 26 cards of your full pack should be identical to the second 26 cards. The other 26 cards are placed in your right jacket pocket with the flashlight. The rubber bands are on the table.

★ Show the faces of the pack to the spectators by spreading them between your hands. The pack will appear to be normal. The fact that it actually contains only 26 cards that are repeated will not be noticed.

"In a moment I will ask three of you merely to think of a card. On no account must you touch them or give me any clue as to the identity or whereabouts of your cards. First, though, I must get rid of half of the pack."

AFTERTHOUGHT

People seldom remember the sequence of events in a card trick, so they won't remember that half the pack is out of sight for a couple of seconds.

★ Count out 26 cards face down onto a pile. Wrap the rubber bands around this packet of cards and place them in a spectator's outside jacket pocket **2**. Be careful not to "flash" the faces of any of the cards as you do this.

Fan the other half of the pack as neatly as you can and hold up the fan in front of the three spectators.

"Think of one of the cards that you can see. Don't tell me – just think of it."

★ When they have thought of their cards, close the fan and hold the cards in your right hand. Put your right hand (still holding the cards) into your jacket pocket, drop the cards, and pick up the other half-pack and the flashlight.

★ Transfer the cards to your left hand and **CASUALLY** put the cards face down on the table. Draw attention to the flashlight by holding it in your right hand for everyone to see. You have successfully switched packets!

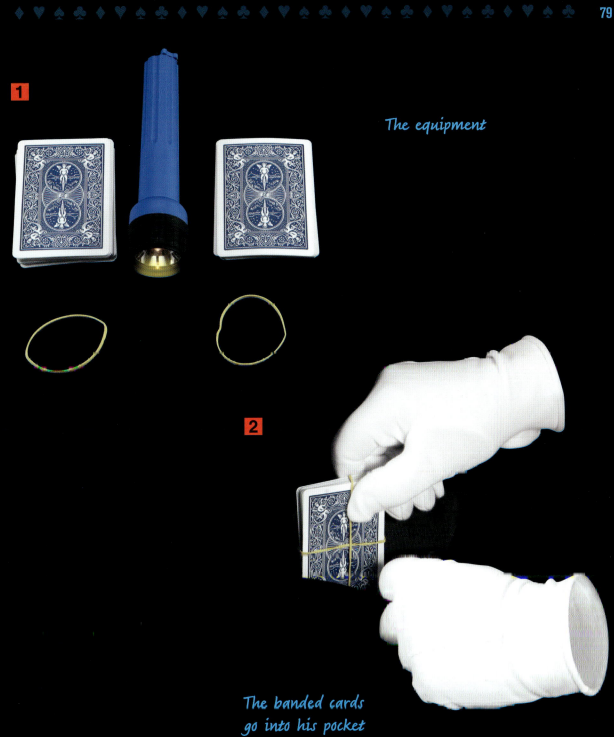

1

The equipment

2

The banded cards
go into his pocket

No one will suspect as long as you treat the cards with indifference and misdirect everyone's attention with the flashlight!

"You are not going to believe this, but this flashlight was given to me by an Alien Magician! No, not an ailing magician – an ALIEN MAGICIAN! He used it for alien abductions. It even works on playing cards – and thoughts! Let me show you…"

★ Shine the flashlight at the forehead of each spectator, asking them merely to think of their cards as you do this. Then shine the light over the half pack of cards on the table for five seconds. Count to five as you do this – then quickly switch off the flashlight. Go over to the fourth spectator and shine the light at his pocket for five seconds – again counting to five. Switch the flashlight off.

"That should do it! Gentlemen, would you please name the cards that you have been thinking of."

★ They name their cards.

★ Ribbon spread the cards that are on the table face up, to show that the cards that they were thinking of have vanished! Have the fourth spectator take the cards out of his pocket, remove the rubber bands and search for the three missing cards. He finds all three cards in the packet that he has been guarding all along!

♥   ♠

AFTERTHOUGHT

This trick leaves you with a normal pack of 52 cards at its completion. You can now perform another trick – if you know one strong enough to cap this one!

♣   ♦

Searching for the three missing cards

STACKED DECK TRICKS

Now for something completely different. You have a new principle to learn that is simplicity itself. Subtle application of this principle will enable you to do dozens of dynamic tricks. Once you have grasped the principle you may even be able to invent a few yourself!

★ Read on and learn some great tricks using the stacked deck principle. Together, these tricks make a great 15-minute card act. Just remember, before you launch yourself upon an audience, you must practice, practice, and then practice...

You will learn how to perform the following tricks:

One in the Middle

Behind my Back

Red Hot Poker

Lucy Locket

Knife Edge

THE STACKED DECK

In the right hands, a stacked deck can perform miracles! At first glance, the cards are completely mixed up. You know, however, the exact order of the 52 cards. Don't panic! It's easier than you think, with just two things to remember.

WHAT YOU DO

★ This is the order of the pre-arranged, or "stacked" deck, beginning with the top card.

A♣ 4♥ 7♠ 10♦ K♣ 3♥ 6♠ 9♦ Q♣ 2♥ 5♠ 8♦ J♣ A♥ 4♠ 7♦ 10♣ K♥ 3♠ 6♦ 9♣ Q♥ 2♠ 5♦ 8♣ J♥ A♠ 4♦ 7♣ 10♥ K♠ 3♦ 6♣ 9♥ Q♠ 2♦ 5♣ 8♥ J♠ A♦ 4♣ 7♥ 10♠ K♦ 3♣ 6♥ 9♠ Q♦ 2♣ 5♥ 8♠ J♦

★ Here's how you memorize the order the cards must follow.

★ First, use the word **CHASED**. The "**C**" stands for **CLUBS**, the "**H**" stands for **HEARTS**, the "**S**" stands for **SPADES** and the "**D**" is for **DIAMONDS**. The pack is arranged so that every fourth card is of the same suit. So the first card will be a ♣, the second a ♥, the third a ♠, the fourth a ♦, the fifth a ♣, the sixth a ♥, and so on.

DID YOU KNOW?

Some decks use four colors for the suits to make it easier to tell them apart.
Black-Spades
Red-Hearts
Blue-Diamonds
Green-Clubs

AFTERTHOUGHT

Read through the five tricks in this section, and practice them all again and again. The five together make a great routine.

★ Remember that each card in the sequence increases by the value of 3. So the first card is an Ace or 1, the next is 4, the next is 7, the next is 10, the next a King, the next a 3, and so on. (Jacks = 11, Queens = 12, and Kings = 13.)

★ So the first card in the pack will be an Ace – the A♣. The second will be a 4 – the 4♥. The third will be a 7 – the 7♠. The fourth – the 10♦. The fifth – the K♣, and so on throughout the pack.

★ Any amount of complete cuts will not disturb the order of the cards. It will merely change the starting point of the 52-card sequence.

★ Say you have cut the 4♣ to the bottom. You know that by advancing the suit sequence, the top card will be a ♥. By advancing the value by 3 you know that the top card is a 7. It is the 7♥!

★ By calculating backwards, the card that is second from bottom is the A♦.

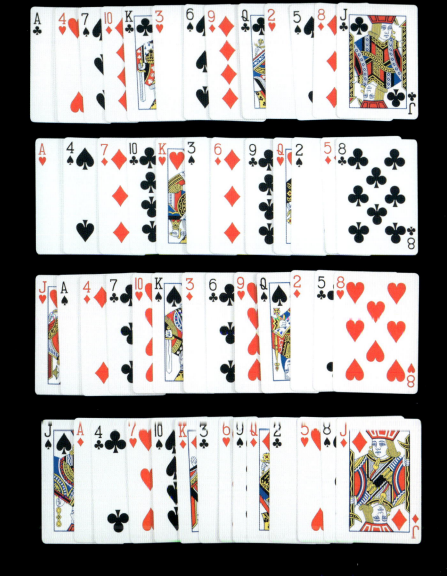

STACKED DECK PRACTICE ROUTINE
...the pack a few times, then look at the bottom card. Name the top card.
Turn it face up and deal it onto the table.
...name the next card before you turn it over. Continue through the entire
pack, attempting to name each card before you turn it over.

TWO FOR ONE

Here are your first two stacked-deck tricks, plus instructions for performing a false shuffle with this loaded deck. One in the Middle is a quick and impressive first trick, while Behind My Back does exactly what you would expect from the name!

ONE IN THE MIDDLE

★ After many shuffles and cuts, you explain that nobody could possibly know what the middle card is. You name it – and then count down to the 26th card and show that you're correct!

★ But how does this work? You can gauge the middle (26th) card in the pack very quickly. It will be the same value and the same color as the bottom card. If, for example, the bottom card is the 9♦, then the middle card in the pack will be the 9♥. If the bottom card is the Q♣, the middle card will be the Q♠, and so on. So simple!

BEHIND MY BACK

★ A spectator chooses a card from the pack while it is being held behind your back. You are able to name it instantly! With practice you will be able to ooparate the oardo at the point that the spectator removes the cards from the pack. Put the top half to the bottom and the bottom half to the top – thus cutting the pack.

★ Secretly glimpse the bottom card as you place the pack on the table. Change to the next suit in the sequence – add three – and there you have it! Don't forget to replace the spectator's chosen card back on top of the pack after the trick so that your setup is reinstated.

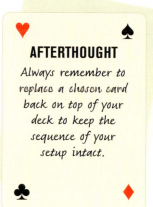

AFTERTHOUGHT

Always remember to replace a chosen card back on top of your deck to keep the sequence of your setup intact.

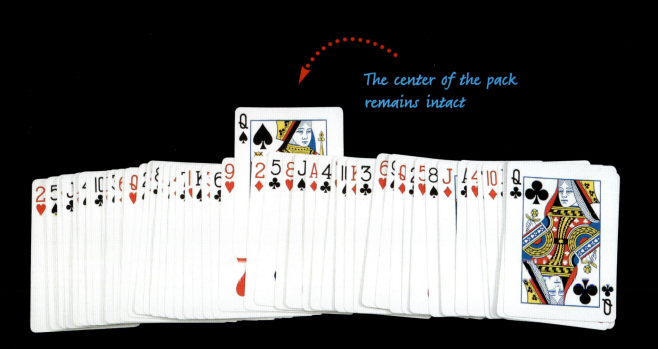

The center of the pack remains intact

STACKED DECK FALSE SHUFFLE

A false shuffle will give your stacked deck tricks an extra lift. This shuffle should be performed in an almost sloppy, offhand way. Hold the pack in your left hand. Push off a few cards from the BOTTOM of the pack into your right hand. Now push off a few cards from the TOP and take them UNDERNEATH the cards in your right hand. Push off some more from the BOTTOM onto the TOP of the right hand cards. Now a few more from the TOP to the BOTTOM. Keep doing this until you have exhausted the pile in your left hand. The order of the pack will still be intact.

DOUBLE TROUBLE

The following part of your routine is fabulous – especially if you have card players in the group who know the importance and rarity of a running flush.

RED HOT POKER

★ Once the pack has been shuffled and repeatedly cut, deal out four poker hands of five cards each. Yours is the fourth hand. Three spectators will ALL be dealt running flushes! Then you turn over your hand to reveal a royal flush!

★ Give the pack a couple of false shuffles and a few cuts until a 2 (any 2) comes to the bottom . Now deal out four poker hands of five cards in each hand. You deal yourself the fourth, eighth, twelfth, sixteenth, and twentieth cards.

★ Get the spectators to turn over their hands one at a time – starting with the person on your left. The suspense builds as each shows a slightly improved hand to the last. Expose your hand last, showing the unbeatable royal flush!

♥   ♠

AFTERTHOUGHT

When you're finished with your stacked deck, gather all the cards up and give them a shuffle to remove all evidence of the setup.

♣   ♦

LUCY LOCKET

★ Three cards are removed from the shuffled deck while it is being held behind your back. The spectator places one in his right jacket pocket, one in his left jacket pocket, and the third in his outside breast pocket. You turn around and name all three cards and successfully locate each one!

★ Ask the spectator to remove a block of three cards. Break the pack at the point that the cards came from and complete the cut. Tell him not to look at the cards and to place the first of his three cards in his right jacket pocket, the next into his left jacket pocket, and the last into his breast pocket.

★ By asking him not to look at the cards it ensures that he keeps them face down – so he will remove the top card first. After glimpsing the bottom card of the pack you can figure out the next three cards in the sequence. You will also know which card is in which pocket! As a "smoke-screen," reveal the cards in 2 – 1 – 3 order! Remember to replace them on the deck in the correct order.

1

False shuffle until a two
comes to the bottom

2

Expose your hand – a
royal flush!

KNIFE EDGE

A spectator slides a table knife into the center of a shuffled pack. He looks at and remembers the card beneath the knife blade. You reveal the name of his card!

DID YOU KNOW?

Items that secretly reflect the identity of cards are called shiners and are often used by crooked gamblers.

WHAT YOU DO

★ The table knife provides the means of secretly glimpsing the card **ABOVE** the knife! The knife is inserted at the numbered corner. It is a moment's work to lift the cards that are above the knife slightly so that you can see a reflected image of the card in the knife blade. Change suits – add three – and you already know the name of the card that he will choose.

★ Immediately take the knife and the cards above it away and place them to one side. Have the spectator look at and remember the card that was underneath the knife blade.

★ Assemble the cards again and give the pack a couple of false shuffles. Run through it and cut the chosen card to the top – then remove it. Ask him to name his choice and finally turn the card over to show that you have managed to achieve the impossible!

★ Place the card back on top and you are ready for another trick.

The image of the card is reflected in the knife blade

FIFTEEN NOVEL
CARD TRICKS

Congratulations! You have come a long way and have worked really hard to have arrived at this point in the book.

★ The skills that you have acquired can now be put to use as you enjoy performing this final collection of dynamic tricks.

★ You will have gathered by now that the great majority of card tricks can be described in very simple terms: a card is chosen, and the magician finds it. Because the plot doesn't vary much, magicians are always striving to discover new and original ways to reveal the chosen card. From the very beginning, this book has tried to show you how to make your tricks different and novel, with unexpected twists and turns along the way so that your audience never gets bored.

★ All the tricks on the following pages have something in common. They are extremely entertaining and delightfully different. Once you have practiced them all, you will be ready to pick out your favorites to try out on your friends.

★ To finish, there is also a crash course in fortune telling with playing cards, and some GOLDEN RULES that you should follow to help you become a truly professional card magician. Have fun!

THE HIGH JUMP

In the first variation of this trick, you throw the pack from your right hand into your left hand and the chosen card dramatically appears, like a flash of lightning! Try it again, dropping the pack onto a table for great results.

WHAT YOU DO

★ Here, the magic of science – air current – causes the chosen card to turn face upwards.

The chosen card is controlled to the top of the pack and then held in your left hand.

The top card is out-jogged **LENGTHWAYS** **1** just under halfway **2**, as the right hand takes the pack away.

The back of your right hand conceals the out-jog.

★ Throw the pack back into your left hand quite sharply. You catch the pack and there – face up on top – is the chosen card. It happens too quickly for the eye to follow. Practice a little and you will soon get the knack!

DID YOU KNOW?

There are a thousand times more tricks with playing cards than all other types of conjuring tricks put together.

NOW TRY THIS ...

★ An alternative version of this trick is to drop the pack onto the table from a height of about two feet. The slipstream causes the out-jogged card to turn over and land on top of the pack **3**, **4** & **5**.

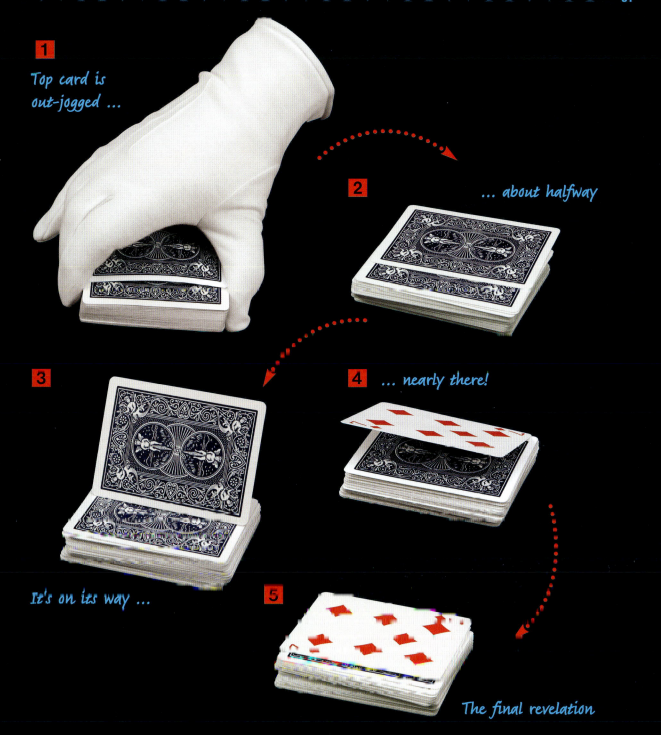

1 Top card is out-jogged ...

2 ... about halfway

3 It's on its way ...

4 ... nearly there!

5 The final revelation

THE PLUNGER

Five cards are inserted into the center of the pack. When they are pushed flush, suddenly four cards pop out the other end! These are pushed in and three cards pop out, and then two, and finally one single card pops out. It is the chosen card!

WHAT YOU DO

★ Shuffle the pack and have one chosen. When it is returned, shuffle it to third from the top. (Undercut – run two cards on top of the chosen card – in-jog the next one, and shuffle off the rest. Undercut at the in-jog and throw on top.)

★ Fan the cards face down in your left hand as neatly as you can. Take the top card off the fan and insert it into the center of the fan, just a little. Take the next card off the top and place it in the pack with just one card from the fan separating it from the card that you have already inserted. Three more cards are now inserted in the same way – each separated by a single card from the fan.

★ The middle card is the chosen one .

AFTERTHOUGHT

This is a very elegant and entertaining way to reveal a chosen card.

★ Close up the fan with the five cards still protruding from the center. Hold them for the spectator to see but without showing him the card faces.

"How many cards are sticking out?"

"Five."

★ Push the cards flush with the pack and you will find that four cards will pop out from the opposite side. These are the four cards that were separating the five that you have just pushed flush.

"How many cards can you see now?"

"Four."

★ Push these flush, and three cards will appear at the other end. Push them flush and two cards come out the other end. Push them flush and a single card will now appear .

★ Have the spectator name his chosen card before you turn your left hand over to show his chosen card projecting from the pack!

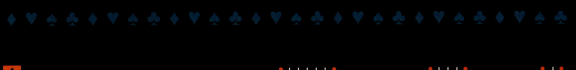

1

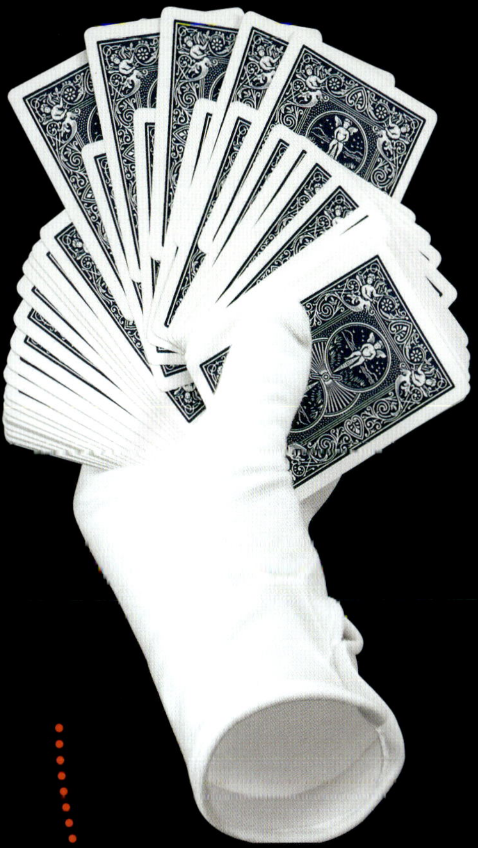

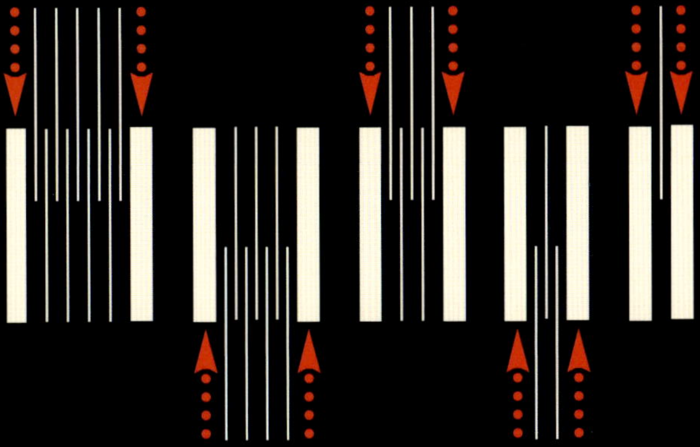

Five cards, each
separated by one card

2

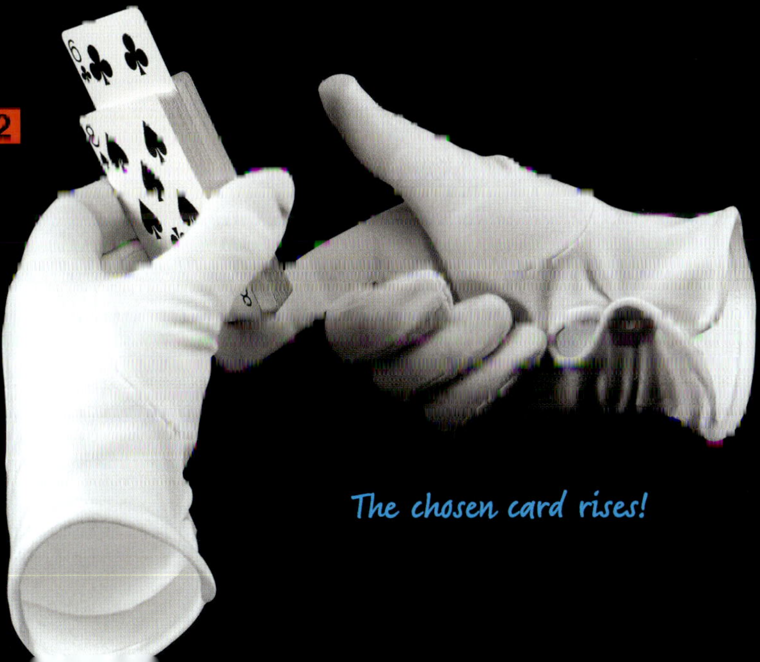

The chosen card rises!

DIAMONDS ARE A GIRL'S BEST FRIEND

This trick always causes amusement. You claim that the lady's chosen card will appear on the bottom of the pack. On inspection, the bottom card is found to be completely blank! The card case is opened and the chosen card is shaken out of it. It is definitely her card – only not in its previous form! She will not have seen anything like this before!

DID YOU KNOW?

Italian playing cards do not have numbers and letters to identify them. You have to do the mathematics yourself!

WHAT YOU DO

★ You need to do a little bit of preparation. Once done it should last you for years. You have to make a blank-faced card. Take any spare card from your supply of duplicates and cover its face with white sticky backed plastic, or simply stick a piece of white paper over the face of the card. Do this as neatly as you can. Insert the finished blank somewhere near the middle of the pack. Also from your supply of duplicate cards, find a high diamond, such as the 9♦.

★ Cut out the nine diamond shapes – then chain link them together with a length of black thread. Glue or tape the end of the thread to the top of your card case on the inside. If you turn the card case mouth downwards, the chain of diamonds should hang out and be visible beneath the case. Now tuck the chain of diamonds back into the case so that they (and the thread) go to the bottom. Put the cards back into the case with the 9♦ from the pack as the top card.

HERE'S HOW TO DO THE TRICK

★ You start by removing the pack from the case. Close the case and place it back on the table. Choose a female spectator and, in the process of having her select a card, force the 9♦.

★ The Cross Hand Force from page 14 suits this trick perfectly. Have her remember her card, put it back in the pack and then thoroughly shuffle the pack.

*Open the case and shake
out the diamond shapes!*

★ Ask her to hide the faces of the cards as she does this.

★ This will ensure that **SHE** doesn't see the faces either –
in case she should shuffle the blank card to the bottom.

★ Take the pack back and look through the cards with the
faces towards yourself. Find the blank card and cut it to the
bottom. Give the cards a couple of false shuffles, retaining the
blank card on the bottom.

★ Place the pack face downwards on top of the card case.

"*I will tap the pack three times and the card that you
chose will travel downwards through the pack and
end up as the bottom card. Watch!*"

★ Tap the pack three times and then dramatically turn it
over. Do a double-take as you see that the card is
completely blank!

"*Oh dear! I must have tapped too hard!
What card did you choose?*"

She tells you the nine of diamonds.

Pick up the card case, open it, and shake out the
nine diamond shapes!

ON THE NOSE!

This novel revelation looks very funny. The chosen card seems to rise up from the shuffled pack, aided by your very own nose.

WHAT YOU DO

★ Control the chosen card to the top of the pack in the course of an overhand false shuffle.

★ Hold the pack in front of your forehead in your left hand.

★ Ask the spectator to name the card that he chose.

★ Bring the pack slowly down in front of your face. Let the top card come in contact with the tip of your nose. Continue lowering the pack.

★ The chosen card will appear to rise up out of the pack – aided by the contact with your nose!

★ When it is about three quarters of the way out, grab it with your right hand and display the chosen card!

♥ ♠ AFTERTHOUGHT

You could also palm the chosen card – give the pack to the spectator to shuffle then stick the chosen card to your forehead while his attention is distracted.

♣ ♦

WINDOW GLEAN

The chosen card is found stuck to the outside of a window – looking in! How on earth can that happen?

WHAT YOU DO

★ This is a nighttime trick – after curtains have been drawn. Secretly stick a duplicate card to your host's window (with a small piece of double-sided sticky tape) so that the face of the card will be seen from inside the room when the curtains are opened. The twin of this one is forced upon the unwitting spectator. It is then shuffled back into the pack and controlled to the top in the course of an overhand false shuffle. Palm the card.

★ State that you are going to throw the cards at the curtains and one card will stick to them. Throw the cards. All the cards fall to the floor. Appear to be disappointed that the trick hasn't worked. Have the spectator name his card out loud. Then ask him to try to find it among the cards that are scattered all over the floor.

★ He fails. (Pocket the palmed card while he is searching fruitlessly.)

★ Say that maybe you threw the cards too hard. Open the curtains to show that his card is stuck to the window. Ask him to pick it off. Watch his amazed expression when he discovers that his chosen card is actually on the OUTSIDE of the window-pane!

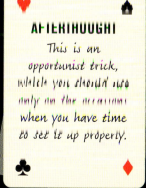

AFTERTHOUGHT
This is an opportunist trick, which you should use only on the occasions when you have time to set it up properly.

THE WHISPERING JOKER

Many magicians will not use an accomplice, but if you know someone you can trust, you can have a lot of fun with this one. A spectator thinks of a card while you are out of the room. Upon your return you instantly name the card!

WHAT YOU DO

★ Get the 10♥, 10♠, or the10♣ on the bottom of the pack. Any one will do. Take the Ace to ten of diamonds from the pack and lay the ten cards face up on the table exactly as shown in the pattern opposite **1**.

Take a close look at the layout. You will notice that the cards are in the same position as the ten pip symbols would be on any 10 value playing card.

Place the balance of the pack face up on the table. Your accomplice should be close to the table. Let's call him Jack. Pick out a lady.

"They say that diamonds are a girl's best friend. I am going to leave the room for a moment. I will be escorted to make sure that I do not eavesdrop. While I am outside I would like you to look at the cards that are spread out on the table and when you are ready, call out the name of the diamond that you like best."

★ You are escorted out of the room (not by your accomplice). The chosen spectator names her card, and you are called back in.

"I have a secret helper in the pack! He is called the Whispering Joker! Hand me the pack, Jack."

★ Jack picks up the pack and hands it to you. In this action he is able to signal the chosen card to you! He just puts his thumb over the corresponding suit symbol of the bottom card. Picture **2** shows him signalling the 7♦.

You now know what the card is so you must act it up for all you are worth! Look through the pack and remove the Joker. Speak to it…

"I'm not entirely sure, but the Whispering Joker seems to think that you are thinking of the seven of diamonds. Is he right?"

♥ ♠ AFTERTHOUGHT

Practice your acting skills before performing this trick. Talk to the Joker; ask it the name of the card; hold it to your ear so that it can ♣ "whisper" to you! ♦

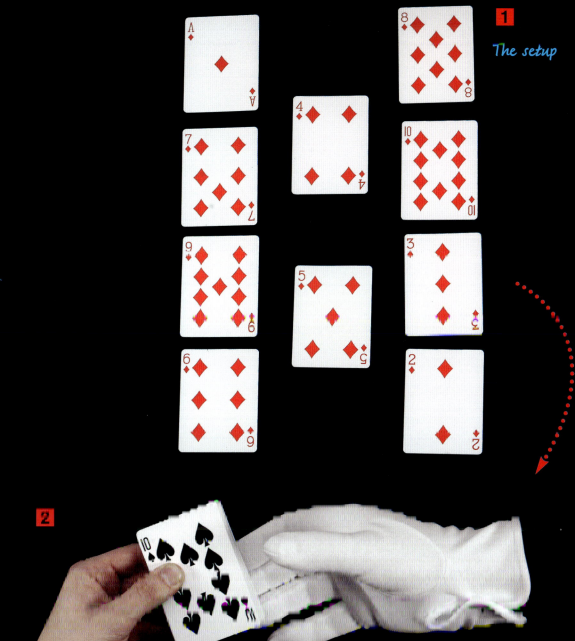

2

UP, UP, AND AWAY

It is a little-appreciated fact that people almost never look up. The keen magician studies anomalies like this and uses them to his own advantage. In this trick, the magician throws the cards into the air and they all drop down to earth again – except one! The chosen card sticks to the ceiling.

WHAT YOU DO

★ This is an opportunist trick: one that you perform only when the conditions are right and the opportunity presents itself. All you have to do is stick a duplicate card on the ceiling of the room where you will be performing.

★ You now merely have to force the twin of this card onto your unsuspecting volunteer. Have it returned and the pack well shuffled, bringing it to the top in the process. Palm it in your right hand. Take the pack in your left hand. Then, without warning, throw the pack up to the ceiling in the proximity of the card that you have previously stuck there. As the cards cascade down again, look up, and then point out the single card that has somehow got stuck to the ceiling!

AFTERTHOUGHT

Add a little more showmanship by insisting that a stepladder is produced to retrieve the chosen card from its lofty position!

THE CALLING CARD

Occasionally you can use a secret duplicate card to great effect. A pack that is a little grubby but still reasonably presentable should never be thrown away. You never know when you may need an odd card or two! Like here, for instance, where the spectator's card vanishes from the pack and is found on the mat outside his front door!

WHAT YOU DO

★ Secretly drop the duplicate card on the doormat as you arrive. Force the card that matches it from the deck. Have it returned to the pack and shuffle it to the top during the course of an overhand false shuffle. Double lift to show the top card and ask the spectator if it is his card. He will, of course, say no. Replace both on top.

★ Start suddenly and say...

"Did you hear that? I'm sure I just heard the door bell! I think there must be someone at the front door!
You had better go and see who it is!"

★ Your host goes to answer the door and finds that the only caller is his chosen card – staring up at him from the front door mat!
You, of course, palm off the duplicate card from the pack and casually drop it, unseen, into your jacket pocket before he returns!

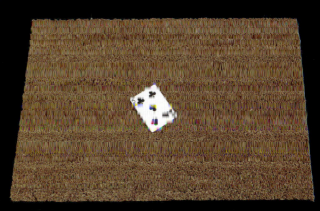

The chosen card is on the doormat!

THE TWIST

This a very quick and effective trick, where the spectator's card is shown to be the only reversed card in the pack. It works well on its own on those occasions when you are asked to perform on demand.

WHAT YOU DO

★ When the chosen card is returned to the pack, control it to the top and keep it there during a couple of overhand false shuffles. You've done this many times before, so you should now be able to do it with your eyes closed!

For ease of explanation, we will assume that the card was the 5♥.

★ Double lift the top two cards, showing them as one and lay it (them) face up on top of the face-down pack. An indifferent card will be showing, say the K♣ 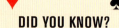. Ask if this is the chosen card. The spectator will say no.

DID YOU KNOW?
The King of Hearts originally had a moustache, but it was lost by poor copying of the original design.

★ Turn your left wrist over so that the pack becomes face up – showing the bottom card – which we will assume is the 2♠.

★ Ask if the 2♠ is the chosen card. Again the spectator will say no **2**.

★ Reach underneath the pack and slide out the K♣ **3**. Turn it over and slide it back again **4**. It will now cover the chosen card and it is safe to turn your left hand back again so that the pack is in a face down position. Cut the pack and complete the cut. This brings the chosen card to somewhere near the center of the pack.

★ Ribbon spread the cards face up to show that there is now one face down card **5**. Have it named, then have the spectator turn it over! Wow!

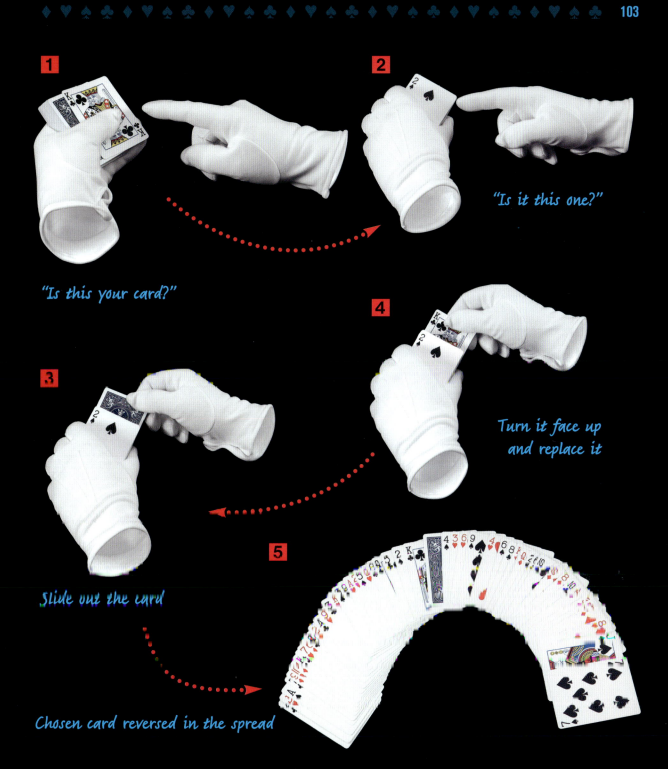

1

"Is this your card?"

2

"Is it this one?"

3

Slide out the card

4

Turn it face up
and replace it

5

Chosen card reversed in the spread

WHAT A COINCIDENCE!

You will need two packs of cards with different back designs for this trick. The spectator chooses one of the packs and selects a card from it. You select a card from the other pack. You both choose identical cards. Our familiar friend the key card is back!

WHAT YOU DO

★ Put both packs of cards on the table in front of the spectator. Ask him to choose a pack and pick it up. You pick up the other one .

"From now on I want you to do exactly as I do. Follow me as best you can! Please shuffle your pack, like this…"

★ Do a simple overhand shuffle. He follows suit. Secretly glimpse the bottom card of your pack as you complete the shuffle. Remember it.

"Now, we've both shuffled our cards, so it must be true that you don't know the order of my cards and I couldn't possibly know the order of yours."

> ♥ ♠
> **DID YOU KNOW?**
> The J♠ and J♥ are drawn in profile, while the rest of the face cards are shown in full face, with the exception of "one eyed Jack," the J♦.
> ♣ ♦

"So – you take my pack and I will take yours. Now remember to do exactly as I do. Take any card from somewhere near the middle of your pack. Look at it, remember it, place it back on top of your pack, then cut the cards and complete the cut. Cut the pack twice more."

★ He follows your actions. The card that you removed and apparently remembered can be ignored. The only card that you must remember is the card that you glimpsed earlier (before you exchanged packs). It is now resting helpfully right above the card that the spectator has just chosen.

"Now, you take my pack and I will take yours. Quickly look through the pack and remove the card that you have chosen, then place it face down on the table, but let me get my card down first! Okay?"

★ When you get his pack, quickly locate your key card and remove the card beneath it. Place it face down on the table.

★ He places his card face down next to yours **2**. Turn his card over, and let him turn over yours. They are the same. What a coincidence **3**!

> ♥ ♠
> **AFTERTHOUGHT**
> With a trick involving a key card, you must ensure all the cuts are complete. Since the spectator is following you, this shouldn't be a problem.
> ♣ ♦

1 *Two packs with diffferent backs are used*

2

3

Both selections are tabled

What a coincidence!

THREE HANDS

Think of the amazing tricks that would be possible if a magician really had three hands! Well, the following trick does use three hands! Three spectators think of cards. You "read their minds" and find all three!

WHAT YOU DO

★ Hand out the pack to be thoroughly shuffled. Take it back and look through it, removing the Joker. While you are doing this, remember the top three cards and their order. Give the pack to another spectator and have him deal out three cards in a row, and then continue to deal onto these three until all the cards have been exhausted. After he has dealt about a dozen cards, tell him he can deal the cards in any order he likes – two on one pile, three on another – it is entirely up to him. This is, of course, a red herring, because your skullduggery has already been done. Your key cards are already in place as the bottom card of each pile. Now you set the scene.

"You shuffled the cards and have done all the dealing and sorting of the cards yourselves. I haven't even touched the cards. Right?"

AFTERTHOUGHT

Similar in effect to Forethought (page 56), the method is different. Here, the pack can be shuffled before you start because no pre-trick set up is required.

★ It isn't right, but they won't remember that you looked through the cards to remove the Joker. Pick three spectators and stand each in front of a pile. Get them to look at the top card and remember it. They are then asked to do complete cuts, to bury their chosen cards in the middle of their packets.

★ Now assemble the packets into one complete pack and cut several times. Thumb through the cards and search for your three key cards. Remove the cards that are beneath them. These are the three chosen cards! Since you have remembered the order of the original three key cards, you now know who owns which card. Very sneaky!

★ Place them face down in front of the three spectators. Have each name their cards and then turn the cards that are in front of them face up.

★ The effect on them will be staggering!

This trick is a lot easier to do than you would imagine. Just get the timing right and you will have a "miracle" on your hands. The spectator discovers that she is actually sitting on the card that she chose!

DID YOU KNOW?

Until August 4, 1960, all packs of cards sold in the United Kingdom. were. sealed with a Government duty wrapper to show that tax had been paid.

WHAT YOU DO

★ A seated spectator chooses a card. You control it to the top and keep it there throughout several false shuffles. Remove any other three cards and place them face up on the floor in front of her and about two feet away from her shoes. Ask if her card is among the three. She assures you that it isn't. Turn the three cards face down. Stand near and to the left of her chair. Tell her that she may point to any of the three cards and it will magically change into her chosen card!

★ **PALM THE TOP CARD NOW!**

★ She points to one of the three cards.

"Please turn it over to see if it has worked."

★ Since she can't quite reach she will lean forward – almost but not quite out of her chair – to turn the card up.

★ Drop the palmed card behind her. It will fall silently onto the seat of the chair and she will sit on it when she reverts to her original position. Obviously the card that she turned over is still not the one that she chose.

"What card did you choose?"

She names it.

"I couldn't have heard! Please stand up and turn around."

★ She does – and finds her chosen card on her seat!

THE MAGIC SPELL

This is quick, effective, and very easy to do, providing that the spectator can spell! He mentally and silently spells out the name of his chosen card as you deal cards face up onto the table. When he has completed his "spell," the next card is the chosen one.

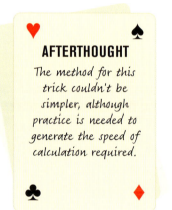

AFTERTHOUGHT

The method for this trick couldn't be simpler, although practice is needed to generate the speed of calculation required.

WHAT YOU DO

★ Have a card freely chosen and returned to the pack. Control it to the top in the usual way. Give the pack a further false shuffle. Fan the faces of the cards towards you. Secretly glimpse the chosen (top) card **1** and then close the fan.

★ Now quickly mentally spell its name by pushing one card at a time from the bottom of the pack into your right hand.

★ For example: If the top (chosen) card was the 6♥, you would spell S - I - X - O - F - H - E - A - R - T - S and then cut the 11 cards to the top of the pack above the chosen card.

★ Carefully explain to the spectator exactly what you want him to do.

"I am going to start dealing the cards face up onto the table, one at a time. You must mentally spell out the name of your card, using each one of the cards that I deal as a letter of your card name. For example, if you are thinking of the Ace of clubs, in your mind (at this point, start to deal the cards from the top of the pack) *you will spell out A - C - E - O - F - C - L - U - B- S. Please shout out "Stop" on the last card of your spell. And don't forget the word 'of'!"*

★ Pick up the cards that you have just dealt and place them back on top of the pack again.

"Are you ready? Here we go..."

★ Start dealing face up cards very slowly. Stop when told. Place the **NEXT** card face down on the spectator's outstretched palm. Ask him to name the card that he is thinking of – then ask him to turn over the card that he is holding!

★ Dynamite!

DID YOU KNOW?

The ornately designed Ace of Spades always carries the card manufacturer's name.

1

Glimpsing the top card

THE PRINCESS CARD TRICK

Five cards are laid face down. You turn your back and ask a spectator to remember one. You turn around, gather up the cards, and put them in your pocket, then remove one card at a time until only one is left. Triumphantly you turn it over to show it is his chosen card!

WHAT YOU DO

★ Secretly place any four cards in your jacket pocket. You are ready to start. Look through the pack and remove any Ace, 2, 3, 4, and 5. The suits do not matter. Lay them face up in a row. They are merely to act as markers.

★ Give the rest of the pack to the spectator and have him thoroughly shuffle the cards, then deal one card on each of the five markers, overlapping them slightly . Instruct him to lift up one of the five cards that he has just dealt while your back is turned. He must remember it, replace it, and then associate it with its marker: say, number 4.

★ Turn around when he has done that and gather up the cards in 1–5 order. Put them in your pocket. Try to keep them separated from the four that you secretly placed there earlier.

DID YOU KNOW?
The Austrian card maker, Piatnik, was founded in 1824 and is still one of the largest manufacturers of playing cards in the world.

"I want you to concentrate hard and think only of the card that you have chosen. I am now going to remove the cards from my pocket, one at a time. The very last card that I remove will, I hope, be the one you are thinking of!" Remove cards one at a time from the four cards that you previously placed there. When the four cards are out, hand them to the spectator and ask him to replace the cards on their markers, casually saying,

"Of course, leave the space for the card that you thought of."

★ You have already put your hand back into your pocket, separating the five cards with your fingers as much as possible.

★ The moment that he leaves a space, you can locate his card and remove it from your pocket. Have him name his card, then slowly and dramatically turn it over to show its face.

AFTERTHOUGHT
This is a very subtle mind-reading trick. And you are in a position to repeat the trick because you still have four cards in your pocket!

THE FAB FOUR

Your shuffling and card control skills transform this easy trick into a spectacular triumph: the four Aces disappear and are found in the spectator's pocket! There are more difficult versions of this trick, but why kill yourself when the effect is exactly the same?!

AFTERTHOUGHT

Tricks featuring the four Aces are always popular with an audience.

WHAT YOU DO

★ The four Aces are laid face up in a row on the table. The rest of the pack is held in your left hand. Ask a spectator to indicate his favorite Ace. While he deliberates over this, secure a little finger break under the top three cards. When he chooses an Ace – say the A♥ – pick it up and lay it face up on the top of the pack **1**.

★ Pick up the other three Aces and place them on top of the A♥. Now reach over with your right hand and pick up the Aces and the three cards above your finger break. Hold the cards in a squared-up packet.

★ Now for the clever part! You are going to show the seven cards as if they were only four! **2**

★ Hold the packet over the rest of the pack so that they cover about half of it. Rest your left thumb on the top Ace **3**.

★ Move your right hand and its cards back to the right again. The top Ace stays put because of the pressure of your thumb **4**.

★ Just before the cards clear the right edge, use them to flip the Ace face down on top of the pack **5**.

★ The three parts of this move should be practiced until they blend into one smooth action.

★ Repeat the turn-over action with the next two Aces – just flipping the cards over. Keep the cards in your right hand squared up so that you do not expose the three extra cards.

★ Drop the packet of four cards on top and flip the last Ace over so that it is also face down. This action looks just the same as the other three times.

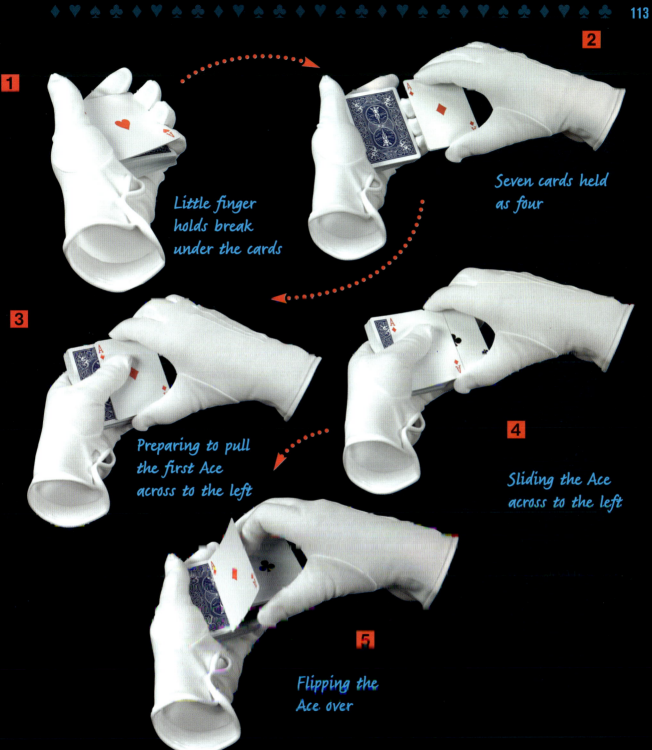

1

Little finger holds break under the cards

2

Seven cards held as four

3

Preparing to pull the first Ace across to the left

4

Sliding the Ace across to the left

5

Flipping the Ace over

★ The order of the cards (from the top) is now: His Ace, followed by three indifferent cards, followed by the other three Aces, then the balance of the pack. Deal the first four cards out in a row from left to right **6**.

The spectator will believe that they are all Aces, when in reality, the only Ace is his chosen one in position 1.

★ The other three Aces are on top of the pack.

★ Overhand false shuffle the pack, keeping the Aces on top.

★ State that you will now deal three odd cards onto each Ace. Deal the first three cards onto pile 1, the next three onto pile 2, and so on.

★ The tableau now looks like picture **7** opposite.

★ Pick up the first pile and turn it over to show his chosen Ace at its face. Take care not to expose the other three cards.

"I am going to put your Ace and the three odd cards into your pocket."

★ Have him clasp his hand over the pocket "for extra security" once the cards are safely in it. Pick up another pile and start to deal the cards face up on the table, counting them as you do.

"One...two...three odd cards...and an Ace."

★ Turn the last card up with a flourish.

"The Ace has disappeared!"

★ Repeat this with the other two piles to show that all three Aces have unaccountably vanished!

★ Have him remove the four aces from his own pocket!

7

Three cards dealt onto each position.

GIVE YOURSELF A HAND!

THE ILLUSION: You clap your hands and the chosen card suddenly appears face up on top of the pack. You will amaze audiences with this intriguing trick and have them believing that you can control the cards with a clap of your hands!

WHAT YOU DO

★ Control the chosen card to the top. Secretly give the top card a slight lengthways bend **1**.

Place the pack on the table in front of you with its long side facing you. Rest your hands on the table about three feet apart and with the palms facing each other. Sweep both hands **RAPIDLY** across the surface of the table so that the palms make a loud "clap" between you and the pack of cards. The slipstream (rush of air) will cause the top card to jump into the air and turn face up on top of the deck in a most startling manner! **2**

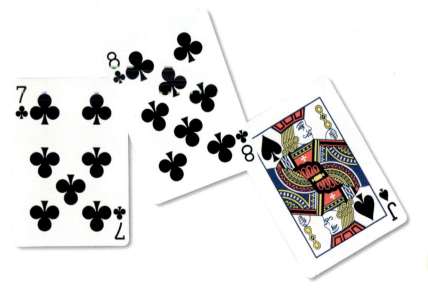

DID YOU KNOW?
The 9 of diamonds is sometimes known as the Curse of Scotland. There are several theories as to how this originated, but none is proven.

1 *The top card is slightly bent*

2 *The chosen card jumps*

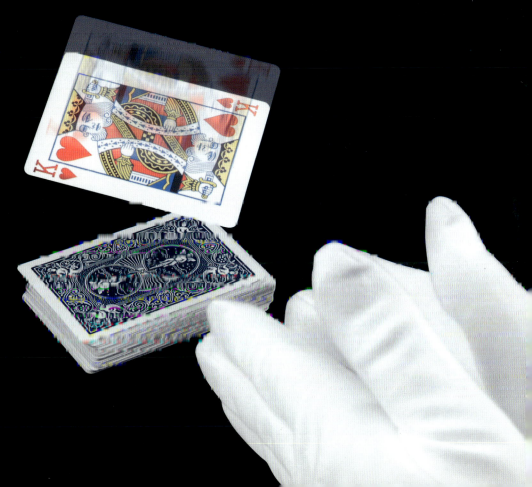

FORTUNE TELLING WITH CARDS

Playing cards have always been used to tell fortunes. When people know that you can do card tricks, they will often ask if you can tell fortunes with the cards. Each card is given a meaning and quality. The lower cards are usually discarded for this purpose. Use your imagination to make up the story as you go along, using the following as guidelines!

HEART VALUES

ACE ♥ Good news in a love letter

KING ♥ Kind man with fair complexion

QUEEN ♥ Generous, loving woman

JACK ♥ Pleasure-loving bachelor

TEN ♥ Good fortune

NINE ♥ The wish card

EIGHT ♥ Invitation to love

SEVEN ♥ Contentment

SPADES VALUES

ACE ♠ Satisfaction in love

KING ♠ An interesting widower

QUEEN ♠ A faithful friend

JACK ♠ Doctor or lawyer

TEN ♠ Long journey

NINE ♠ Some disappointment

EIGHT ♠ Slight health worry

SEVEN ♠ Unexpected change

Examples of card fortunes

DIAMONDS VALUES

ACE ♦ Marriage offer – ring

KING ♦ Interesting older man

QUEEN ♦ Wdow or gossip

JACK ♦ A helpful official

TEN ♦ An enjoyable journey

NINE ♦ Long-awaited news

EIGHT ♦ Amorous journey

SEVEN ♦ A happy child

CLUBS VALUES

ACE ♣ Very good luck

KING ♣ Dark, friendly man

QUEEN ♣ Dark, affectionate woman

JACK ♣ Athletic lover

TEN ♣ Ease and prosperity

NINE ♣ Unexpected legacy

EIGHT ♣ Lucky in love

SEVEN ♣ Financial success

AFTERTHOUGHT
Knowledge of
the meanings of the
cards can only
enhance your card
trick commentary.

YOUR PERFORMANCE

Here are some tips to consider when you are performing in front of an audience and some warnings about traps to avoid. Time taken preparing for your performance will reap lots of benefits and make you feel – and look – confident.

PRESENTATION

★ You should never perform the same trick twice to the same group on the same day. To be forewarned is to be forearmed. If they know what is going to happen they stand more chance of finding out how the trick is done. You must try to make your tricks acceptable for their entertainment value alone.

★ Never perform for too long. Half an hour is more than enough. Leave your audience wanting more! Half a dozen tricks are all that you will need.

★ Choose your six tricks carefully so that they contrast with each other as much as possible.

★ Save your best trick until last.

★ Be flexible and self-critical. Your favorite trick might not be the one that your audiences enjoy the most!

★ Pick tricks that seem to suit your personality best.

★ Handle your volunteer assistants with care and politeness. Never be over familiar, especially with a member of the opposite sex.

★ Keep up the practice!

★ Enjoy yourself – if you look as if you're having fun, your audience will as well.

AFTERTHOUGHT

Never be afraid to alter the commentary suggested here. They are someone else's words and may not suit the way that you talk. Be original!

YOUR APPEARANCE

The days when magicians wore flowing robes and long pointed conical hats have gone forever, thank goodness! These days magicians may appear wearing all sorts of unusual gear, but there are a few golden rules to follow when you are performing in public.

SOME RULES

★ You must always be as well, if not better, dressed than the best-dressed person in the room.

★ If you are charging for your services, you should always look as if you do not really need the money!

★ Make sure that your clothes are always clean, well-pressed and in a state of good repair.

★ And that goes for your shoes, too! Don't forget to give them a really thorough polish!

★ When you are performing, the spectators will be watching your hands all the time, so they must be clean and your fingernails well-manicured.

AFTERTHOUGHT

It is always worth spending an extra five minutes checking your appearance before a performance.

DON'T PANIC!

Believe it or not, even the very best, most expert magicians occasionally make mistakes. This section offers some advice on how to handle that inevitable and potentially embarrassing situation.

COVERING UP

★ Fortunately, you have one terrific "Ace" up your sleeve! In almost every trick that you present, you do not ever tell the audience what you are going to do until you have actually done it.

★ So, if you make a mistake halfway through a trick and it seems impossible that you will be able to bring it to a successful conclusion, you can quickly change direction and give the trick a different ending. The spectators will be none the wiser. This technique becomes easier as you become more accomplished as a performer, but don't be put off by your inexperience. Be bold and bluff your way through. You will soon learn to cover your mistakes.

★ If the worst comes to the worst and you really do mess up, the best policy is to own up to your mistake and start again. The spectators will appreciate your honesty and they will realize that you are only human after all!

★ Another invaluable tip is to always use clean playing cards. If you try to manipulate worn-out or sticky playing cards you are just asking for trouble, and mistakes will surely follow.

★ When performing, try not to handle your pack of cards for more than half an hour at a time. This will keep them fresh and make them last longer.

DID YOU KNOW?

Tarot cards were invented in Renaissance Italy in the early fifteenth century.

CREATING MAGIC

★ This is an art. What is common to all inventors of magic tricks is the solid background of the basic magical principles.

★ By the time you have reached the end of this book, you will have realized that it is the presentation of a trick, rather than the method of achieving it, that makes a successful magician.

★ A really competent magician will often be able to perform a trick for someone who thinks he or she knows the secret of the trick, but who is still fooled by the sheer skill of the magician's performance.

★ Remember that the public's memory is short! Most people might think they know a trick, but they soon forget how it's done and are entertained and entranced again when they see it performed in a novel and professional way.

★ The methods described in the book are really quite simple, but by the time they have been dressed up with presentation, finesse and humor, magical illusions are created.

★ Now you have been let in on the secrets of how to be a fantastic magician ■ it's up to you to carry on the illusion!

ABOUT THE AUTHOR

Honored by his colleagues by elevation to Membership of the INNER MAGIC CIRCLE (London) with GOLD STAR (the highest award that a magician can receive), Jon has been a world-class performer for over 30 years.

JON'S PERFORMANCES

Jon's magical talents have taken him around the world many times over, to a dazzling array of night clubs, hotels, cruise liners, television shows, corporate events, and society parties. His tours have taken him to almost every town in Africa, South Africa, Swaziland, Botswana, and Tanzania.

He recently performed for the citizens of Pitcairn Island and Easter Island. One of his most memorable experiences was being invited into a Zulu witch doctor's hut to exchange tricks!

He has also performed before the British Royal family at a Christmas party at Windsor Castle, where he magically "read" the mind of Prince Charles!

JON'S INTERESTS

Jon is a prolific writer and has over 30 published books to his credit on subjects ranging from astrology to balloon modeling. Future projects include books on astronomy and space travel.

His hobbies include traveling, food, backgammon, astronomy, and origami – but not necessarily in that order!

Jon lives with his wife, Suzy, in Surrey, England, and in Almoradí on the Costa Blanca, Spain.

DID YOU KNOW?
Female magicians were not admitted to the Magic Circle until members voted in favor of their inclusion in 1991.

GLOSSARY OF TERMS

ARM SPREAD

A flourish whereby you ribbon spread the cards along your outstretched arm (page 38).

BACK

The design on the back of the playing card.

CARD APEX

A flourish whereby you spread a pack of cards across a table, then flip them over using a playing card (page 36).

CARD SPREAD

The act of spreading out the cards for a choice to be made.

CROSS HAND FORCE

A subtle method of getting a spectator to choose a card or cards, the identity of which you already know. You "force" their choice (page 14).

CUTTING THE PACK AND COMPLETING THE CUT

To cut the pack is to divide it into two piles. The cut is completed by reassembling the pack. The top half is now the bottom half and the bottom half is now at the top.

DOUBLE-LIFT

The action of lifting two cards from the top of the pack, keeping them perfectly aligned, and showing them as if they were only one card (page 44).

FACE DOWN

The card's back design is shown, concealing the card's identity.

FACE UP

A card's identity is shown.

FINGER BREAK

The method of inserting the tip of your little finger into the cards to mark a position in the pack (page 44).

FINGER SPREAD

A nice flourish whereby you perform a table spread and turn the cards over using your index finger to ride the crest of the wave (page 36).

GLIDE

A sleight enabling you to show a card to the audience and then exchange it for a completely different card during the process of dealing (page 16).

IN-JOG

During an apparently genuine shuffle, this is the action of overlapping a single card inwards, towards your body by about $3/4$ of an inch (page 8).

KEY CARD

This is a card, the identity and location of which you know, but the spectator doesn't. It is used to help you locate the spectator's chosen card (page 49).

LENGTHWAYS SPREAD

The act of spreading the cards in a line across the table by the short end of the cards (page 38).

MISDIRECTION

This is the art of distracting the spectator's attention either physically or mentally and is a common ploy used extensively in all branches of the magic arts.

ONE-WAY CARDS

Playing cards that have a back design that is not geometrical (e.g., a picture of a dog). Have all the dogs the right way up. Turn one dog design upside down and shuffle the pack. If you now spread through the pack the one card that you have just turned around will stick out like a sore thumb! Nineteen of the card

FACES also have a one-way design (page 74).

OUT-JOG

The reverse of an in-jog. The single card is overlapped by about $3/4$ of an inch on the side of the pack furthest away from you.

OVERHAND SHUFFLE

The traditional way used to mix up (change the order of) the cards (page 8).

OVERHAND SHUFFLE CARD CONTROL

During the course of an apparently genuine shuffle you use your skill to control a card or cards to a position in the pack that suits the trick that you are performing (page 8)

PACK OR DECK

A complete set of 52 cards

PACKET

A group of cards fewer than 52 is referred to as a packet.

PALMING

The act of secretly stealing a card or cards from the pack and concealing them in the palm of your hand (page 54).

RIBBON SPREAD

The act of spreading the cards in a line across the table (page 7).

RIFFLE SHUFFLE

A spectacular way of mixing up the cards (page 32).

TABLE SPREAD AND TURNOVER

The act of spreading the cards in a line across the table (say face up) then flipping them over so that they all become face down (page 36).

UNDERCUT

This cut is performed with the cards held in your hands. The bottom part of the pack is removed. This is called undercutting.

WATERFALL CASCADE

A flashy finish to a riffle shuffle (page 34).

ACKNOWLEDGMENTS

Written by Jon Tremaine
Edited by Pat Hegarty and Lisa Regan
Creative direction by Tony Potter
Photography by Paul Noble Studios
Designed by Clare Barber and Sue Rose

All inquiries should be addressed to:
Barron's Educational Series, Inc.
250 Wireless Boulevard
Hauppage, NY 11788
www.barronseduc.com

ISBN-13: 978-0-7641-6014-1
ISBN-10: 0-7641-6014-1
Library of Congress Control Number
2006932162
Printed in China
9 8 7 6 5 4 3 2 1